Souls Knit Together

Souls Knit Together: Thirty-One Lessons on Friendship from David and Jonathan

Copyright © 2024 Benjamin Szumskyj. All rights reserved.

Pronomian Publishing LLC
Chatsworth, GA 30705

ISBN: 979-8-9851529-8-2

Publisher grants permission to reference short quotations (fewer than 300 words) in reviews, magazines, newspapers, websites, or other publications. Request for permission to reproduce more than 300 words can be made at **www.pronomianpublishing.com/contact**

Scripture quotations taken from the (NASB®) New American Standard Bible®, Copyright © 1960, 1971, 1977, 1995 by The Lockman Foundation. Used by permission. All rights reserved. lockman.org.

Cover Design: Daniel Kaplan

SOULS KNIT TOGETHER

To my brother in Messiah, James

CONTENTS

Introduction: The Foundation of Friendship 1
Day 1: Becoming a Jonathan ("YHWH has Given") 7
Day 2: A Friend that Honours Their Parents (1 Samuel 13:3) 9
Day 3: A Friend that is Faithful to YHWH (1 Samuel 14:6) 13
Day 4: A Friend that Influences (1 Samuel 14:7) 15
Day 5: A Friend that is Willing to Get their Hands Dirty
(1 Samuel 14:13) 19
Day 6: A Friend Sees the Danger of Short-sighted Oaths
(1 Samuel 14:29) 23
Day 7: A Friend is Willing to Accept Consequences
(1 Samuel 14:43) 27
Day 8: A Friend Works with YHWH (1 Samuel 14:45) 31
Day 9: A Friend is Respected by Others (1 Samuel 14:45) 35
Day 10: A Friend Acknowledges that Friends Have Other
Friends (1 Kings 5:1, 7) 39
Day 11: A Friend Knits Their Soul to Their Friend's Soul
(1 Samuel 18:1) 43
Day 12: A Friend Loves Their Friend as They Love Themselves
(1 Samuel 18:2) 45
Day 13: A Friend is Covenantal in their view of Friendship
(1 Samuel 18:3) 49
Day 14: A Friend Shares Resources with their Friend
(1 Samuel 18:4) 51
Day 15: A Friend Delights in their Friend (1 Samuel 19:1) 55
Day 16: A Friend Speaks well of their Friend (1 Samuel 19:4) 59
Day 17: A Friend is a Voice of Reason for their Friend

(1 Samuel 19:6) 61
Day 18: A Friend finds Favour in their Friend (1 Samuel 20:3) 63
Day 19: A Friend is willing to Serve their Friend
(1 Samuel 20:4) 67
Day 20: A Friend is Unwilling to Lie (1 Samuel 20:9) 71
Day 21: A Friend will Lay Down their Life for their Friend
(1 Samuel 20:13) 73
Day 22: A Friend Keeps their Vows (1 Samuel 20:17) 77
Day 23: A Friend Grieves over their Friend's Misfortune
(1 Samuel 20:34) 81
Day 24: A Friend has Long-term Vision of their Families
being Together (1 Samuel 20:42) 83
Day 25: A Friend Encourages in YHWH (1 Samuel 23:16) 87
Day 26: A Friend Keeps their Vows (1 Samuel 23:18) 91
Day 27: A Friend Dies doing what YHWH has Called
them to do (1 Samuel 31:2) 95
Day 28: A Friend Laments (2 Samuel 1:17) 99
Day 29: A Friend will Recall a Friend Righteously
(2 Samuel 1:18-27) 103
Day 30: A Friend will show Kindness to a Friend's Family
(2 Samuel 9:1-8) 107
Day 31: A Friend is an Individual After YHWH's heart
(Acts 13:22) 111
Conclusion: Faith and Friendship 115
Appendix 1: The Gospel of Messiah Yeshua 119
Appendix 2: On Mentorship in Christianity 123
Author's Biography 127

INTRODUCTION
THE FOUNDATION OF FRIENDSHIP

YHWH—Your First Friend (Mark 12:29-30; John 15:15)

Establishing or strengthening a biblical friendship begins with recognizing the following truth: *divinity is your foundation, not humanity.* In Matthew 7:24-27, Yeshua[1] the Messiah made the following statement:

> Therefore everyone who hears these words of Mine and acts on them, may be compared to a wise man who built his house on the rock. And the rain fell, and the floods came, and the winds blew and slammed against that house; and yet it did not fall, for it had been founded on the rock. Everyone who hears these words of Mine and does not act on them, will be like a foolish man who built his house on the sand. The rain fell, and the floods came, and the winds blew and slammed against that house; and it fell—and great was its fall.
> —Matthew 7:24-27

---

[1] I have chosen to use the Hebrew name "Yeshua" over Jesus and the personal name of God "YHWH" over just the title of God because these restored names are more familiar to those in the Messianic and Pronomian assemblies.

In this parable, Yeshua remarked that anyone who puts His words into practice "may be compared to a wise man who built his house on the rock" (Matthew 7:24). Similarly, earlier in Scripture, King Solomon taught, "By wisdom a house is built" (Proverbs 24:3). Thus, in order to build a house, it is necessary to have a strong foundation or "rock." But what is that rock? The prophet Samuel, preserving the prayer of Hannah, describes this type of rock when he wrote that nowhere in this world "is there any rock like our God" (1 Samuel 2:2). The prophet Isaiah added that YHWH would one day lay down a "costly cornerstone for the foundation, firmly placed" (28:16). Centuries later, after Yeshua had been crucified on a skull-shaped hill and emerged alive from a tomb carved from rock, the apostle Paul confirmed that this "rock was Christ" (1 Corinthians 10:4).

So, what does this all mean? Well, when building your house (that is, yourself), you must build upon a foundation that is flawless (cf. Mark 8:34). Your wife or husband cannot serve as that foundation, and neither can your children, community, profession, or (especially) anything the world offers. All are capable of falling and, yes, failing you. Therefore, YHWH must be your foundation. I learned that the hard way, as while I believed (even taught) that YHWH was my sole foundation, He clearly was not. Otherwise, I would not have descended into such darkness when my parents divorced. (At that time, my earthly father was more of a foundation than my Father in Heaven.)

YHWH alone completes you, and to confess anything else diminishes the sovereignty of YHWH in your life. King Solomon was correct when he said that wisdom is needed in building a house, but too many of us use worldly wisdom when doing so (cf. James 3:15). This is because, according to the world, we are told to build ourselves upon our own efforts and to never prioritize YHWH first. Scripture, the mouthpiece of YHWH, declares the opposite.

Priority and perspective are a problem that has existed since the Garden of Eden. People (and I am including many Christians here) prefer their own *preferences* over the *principles* of YHWH. Their desire is to please themselves and others, rather than prioritize God the Father, Son, and Spirit. YHWH does not come first for them. They desire to look down at YHWH, not up at Him. This should not be! He is the beginning (John 1:1), He enacted the beginning (Genesis 1:1), and He is to be *your* beginning (2 Corinthians 5:17). He is why you and the world exist. Why would a Christian look to the world as their foundation instead of looking to YHWH?

I am reminded of a conversation I had with an Amish minister when I visited Ohio, USA. He said that one of the reasons he and his Amish community separated themselves from the outside world was because, in his words, "all the world does is distract us from God." "Everything in the world," he reinforced, "is to distract and detract from God." Despite my disagreement with aspects of Amish interpretation, I share his sentiments here. I also think of the Hebrews in the desert wanderings during the Exodus. Despite having very little, they were never closer to YHWH because they were utterly dependent on Him. That is unlike today, where believers live in world that insists on being solely independent. We should recall the words of the beloved disciple in 1 John 2:15-17:

> Do not love the world nor the things in the world. If anyone loves the world, the love of the Father is not in him. For all that is in the world, the lust of the flesh and the lust of the eyes and the boastful pride of life, is not from the Father, but is from the world. The world is passing away, and also its lusts; but the one who does the will of God lives forever.
> —1 John 2:15-17

Do not let people or the world be your foundation.

Humanity—Your Other Friends (Mark 12:31; 1 John 2:7-11)

Once we recognize that YHWH must be our only foundation, we can then grasp a second important truth: *prioritizing our love for YHWH enables us to more effectively love others as we love ourselves.* We are commanded to love all of humanity, but there is an order in how we are to love others according to Scripture. If married, our husband or wife must come first. Through marriage, we are made "one flesh" (Genesis 2:23–24). Then, we are to love our children (Psalm 127:3; Malachi 2:15), then our family (1 Timothy 5:8), followed by fellow believers (Romans 12:9-10; Galatians 5:13; 1 John 4:7), and unbelievers (and this includes enemies, Matthew 5:43-48; don't forget that!). They are all to receive love, but each is to receive love in a certain order and in accordance with the nature of the relationship.

We all have friends, with some having more friends than others, but it's the quality of friendships that matters more than the quantity. These friends can range from those that are local to international, in person and afar. Some friends have been known for years; others are just developing. When it comes to friends, they can be found among family members as much as fellow believers in the local assembly. The best of friends are those bound in their love for Messiah Yeshua as their Lord and Saviour. This is true fellowship, true spiritual communion. While some may argue for the value of friendships with unbelievers, in reality, as demonstrated in the Scriptures, the depth of a friendship between two believers makes relationships without a foundation in YHWH seem shallow by comparison. The fruit of an unequally yoked friendship will always be lacking. The New Testament mentions many different types of love using the Greek language, but the type of love most relevant to this devotional is *phileo*. This type of love embodies the qualities of friendship, affection, generosity, and like-mindedness. However, friendship can often be unusual in the sense that you can know someone, but not really *know* them. (Sadly, some believers have a similar relationship with YHWH.) You could call a person a friend, and even see them each week at the local assembly and in your mid-week study group, but they are not so much a friend in the sense that you "love them as yourself." Such love is close, but not too close. For such relationships, you may prefer the word "acquaintance" or "colleague." You might have mutual interests and shared history, but even then, there are boundaries. Some of those boundaries are healthy, but they reveal a limit to the love you give or show them. Scripture reveals a tension in which we are encouraged to foster a sense of closeness and intimacy among fellow believers, viewing ourselves as integral parts of the Body of Messiah (Romans 7:4; 1 Corinthians 10:16; Ephesians 4:12) and nurturing a daily community as brothers and sisters in Messiah (Acts 2:46-47). However, it is equally important, as mentioned earlier, to maintain the right order of priorities, ensuring that we do not invest more time into one another than into YHWH, our spouses, and our families. Nevertheless, truth be told, Christians stumble in the same way that unbelievers do. We have lots of friends, but few if any "real" friends. We know lots of people, but we don't *know* them.

Souls Knit Together is a devotional that I hope and pray will address this problem and strengthen the journey of sanctification. I am by no means an expert on friendship and am myself a work in progress being the type of friend written of in Scripture. However, I remain committed to the will of YHWH and optimistic that friendships like those described in Scripture do exist. Over the month, each day will share a biblical insight and end with a challenge to not only be a hearer (*akroatēs*) with a question shaped by the Word, but to be a doer (*poiētēs*) of the Word (cf. James 1:22-25).[2] The challenges are not prescriptive, but are intended to be meditated upon and applied in accordance with the Holy Spirit.

The model for biblical friendship used in the devotional is that of Jonathan and David (1-2 Samuel). I will focus on Jonathan, as even though his presence in the Scriptures is brief, there is much to glean from his life that teaches us about the heart of friendships. It is my intention to be true to the intent and context of the verses and passages cited, while also integrating other passages from the Scriptures as a whole. Any good that comes from this devotional, I attribute to YHWH. May it be to His glory My life is not about how great I am; it's about knowing the great I AM. He is our greatest friend and He will bless us according to His will.

May He bless you as you aspire to become a friend worthy of knitting a soul into (cf. 1 Samuel 18:1)!

Soli Deo Gloria and Tota Scriptura
Benjamin Szumskyj
Western Australia, 2023

---

[2] I have chosen these Greek words in order to capture the spirit of language familiar to those redeemed Jew and Gentiles of the first century AD. The Epistle of James (Jacob) was an invaluable primer for sanctification.

DAY 1
BECOMING A JONATHAN ("YHWH HAS GIVEN")

It would be difficult to find in the Scriptures a friendship more intimate and well-known than that between Jonathan and David. While we do see strong friendships between men like the apostle Paul and Luke the historian (Colossians 4:14), all the way to Yeshua and the apostle John (John 20:2), the friendship between Jonathan and David has remained the greatest example of what it means to be a friend to another human being. Jonathan, an Israelite and son of King Saul, became friends with David, great grandson of Ruth and Boaz and soon-to-be king. Both men were teenagers when they came to know one another, but they had a maturity that forged a friendship that has echoed throughout the history of the Assembly. Their example of true friendship blesses us with enduring lessons, even thousands of years later.

Those with depraved minds have claimed the two men were in a homosexual relationship, yet Scripture is clear in its condemnation of this abominable practise (Genesis 19:1–13; Leviticus 18:22; 20:13; Romans 1:26–27; 1 Corinthians 6:9). Jonathan and David were men who loved one another as brothers in the faith; it was not superficial, but uniquely deep (cf. 2 Samuel 1:26). Their friendship was both physical and spiritual in nature, and they invested into one another's lives not because they were born into the same family but by choice and intentionally. They were not bound by familial expectation or pressure, but rather, emulated a love that YHWH first spoke of and then would later be exampled in the life of His Son, Yeshua the Messiah.

Jonathan, then, has become a biblical model of what a friend should be for believers of every generation. His life, from his actions and deeds to his thoughts and words, demonstrates what a loving friendship should be between one believer and another. David benefited deeply from this friendship, and he demonstrates what it means to be a beloved friend. Today, we are living in a world where friendships are more sporadic than stationary, virtual than physical, frivolous than fundamental. Sadder still, there are those that desire friendships, who extend themselves in hoping to establish a reciprocal love, but are met with excuses or unmet expectations. Friends are sweet, but take much work, much like the bees that gives us honey.

The life of Jonathan, though, gives us a model of friendship that evokes hope. His name from the Hebrew means "YHWH has given." This is poetic, for in such a name we are given a picture of what a biblical friendship is: *a gift from YHWH*. He desires us to have friends. Friendships are the first steps towards a relationship between man and woman and the first steps towards biblical brotherhood (1 Peter 2:17) or sisterhood (cf. Ruth 1:16-17).

Expect that you will meet a Jonathan. In the meantime, prepare *to be a Jonathan* for another.

Akroartes and Poietes: What is your definition of friendship? Does your definition align with Scripture? Pray today that you might become a friend to a fellow believer, and pray that YHWH will connect you with a new friend during this season of your life.

DAY 2

A FRIEND THAT HONOURS THEIR PARENTS
(1 SAMUEL 13:3)

It is one of the commandments that even unbelievers have heard about: "Honour your father and your mother, that your days may be prolonged in the land which the LORD your God gives you" (Exodus 20:12). So important was this command, it was repeated not only by Yeshua (Matthew 15:4, 19:9) but also His disciples (Ephesians 6:2). It would be fair to state, then, that regardless of your family situation and upbringing, you are commanded to honour parents.

For some believers, this isn't just easy to fulfill; it is a joy to do so. Their upbringing was both biblical and positive, and they have nothing but love and respect for both parents—or, if they grew up in a single-parent family, their father or mother. Honouring them is not a command they struggle with, and they do so in a variety of ways. Honouring them is done in person, from a distance, and in word and in deed.

However, for other believers, fulfilling this command is not so easy. In fact, it can be nearly impossible. Generations of fathers and mothers have neglected to love their children, to the point that some have been abusive, distant, or emotionally neglectful. For some, honouring their parents or parent means rationalising the irrational, and the emotional toll is too much to bear. Yet, all things are possible with YHWH, and not in a Hallmark movie way. We are called to forgive others, not forget, and this act is a reconciliation in the heart, not in person. A believer can honour their parents from a distance by forgiving them and praying for their salvation. If they were dishonourable, you can be honourable in your character and conduct in order for your own children to emulate that (if you are married and have a family).

Jonathan is a believer who would have been more comfortable in the second group of believers I just described. Scripture barely speaks of his mother Ahinoam (1 Samuel 14:50), yet his father Saul is spoken of several times. Scripture depicts Saul as a man of anger, inconsistent faith, and sporadic in his acts of love. Yet, despite his father's flawed character, Jonathan chose a different path. He chose the path of honour. While he had every reason and right to declare a victory to be his and his alone, he honoured his father and gave him the glory (1 Samuel 13:3-4). He did not seek his own fame, but respected his household and the order of authority. He found peace in knowing that YHWH knew of His victory, and that's all that mattered to him.

Be *and* seek a friend that honours their parents—a friend who is accountable for their own actions and words. It has been said that for every finger pointed by a hand, there are three fingers pointing back. In reflecting on my own life, my father, an unbeliever who did provide for my mother and I as a family, did not demonstrate or express a love that a husband and father should give as the head of the household. When he walked out on us and committed adultery, he inflicted an emotional wound that bears scars today. As a believer, though, I am commanded to forgive him. In forgiving him, I honour him. I honour him by acknowledging the past good he did, praying for his salvation, and not speaking evil or lies against him.

The example of Jonathan reveals a friend worth befriending. If a person can honour their parents, regardless of their past—whether it was painful or positive—they demonstrate an honour worth emulating.

A Friend that Honours Their Parents (1 Samuel 13:3)

Akroartes and Poietes: Do you honour your mother and father? How so? If they have passed, do you honour their memory? If relevant to your circumstances, honour your parent(s) by praying for their salvation and "forgiv[e them]… just as God in Christ also has forgiven you" (Ephesians 4:32).

DAY 3

A FRIEND THAT IS FAITHFUL TO YHWH (1 SAMUEL 14:6)

Truth be told, as a Christian, your friendships should primarily be with fellow believers. This is not to say that you can't or shouldn't have unbelieving friends, but in seeking out a new friendship or to strengthen an existing one, you must share the same foundation with them. Otherwise, you risk sinking into quicksand. You should both believe that Yeshua is your Lord and Saviour. You should both declare to "love the Lord your God with all your heart, and with all your soul, and with all your mind, and with all your strength" (Mark 12:30). Your faith is what should bind you in being faithful to the one who is always faithful to you. As hymnist Thomas O. Chisholm wrote, "Great is Thy faithfulness! Great is Thy faithfulness! Morning by morning new mercies I see; all I have needed Thy hand hath provided, Great is Thy faithfulness, Lord unto me!"

Jonathan was such a friend. He was faithful to YHWH and believed in His faithfulness. In 1 Samuel 14:6 we read, "Then Jonathan said to the young man who was carrying his armor, 'Come and let us cross over to the garrison of these uncircumcised; perhaps the Lord will work for us, for the Lord is not restrained to save by many or by few.'" Jonathan understood that YHWH was sovereign and that, in His lovingkindness, He created us with permissive wills. (I say permissive will, rather than free will, for our wills are not so free as to earn or undo the work of the Lord and save ourselves apart from Him. YHWH has permitted us a will, and we are not free to do everything.)

Jonathan was faithful to YHWH, for He had always been faithful to Him and his people. Jonathan knew YHWH was good and in control. To declare openly that "the Lord will work for us... for the Lord is not restrained" reveals a believer who knows that YHWH is the same yesterday, today, and tomorrow (cf. Hebrews 13:8). He and His Word do not change. It reveals a faith not primarily in those made in the image of YHWH, but in YHWH Himself, first and foremost. As a beloved friend, you do not want a believer just in thought, but a believing friend in thought and deed. You want a friend who not only talks the talk, but walks the walk; a doer of the Scriptures, not just a hearer (James 1:22). It is humbling for a beloved friend to have faith in you, but humans being humans, we can and will fail one another. YHWH, however, will never fail us, and our faith must be in Him.

Jonathan knew that David would always put his faith in YHWH first, and David knew the same of his friend Jonathan. A friend whose faith in humanity comes before divinity is a person whose priorities are clearly wrong and in need of immediate correction. YHWH first, then others. A friend who loves YHWH supremely is a friend who has a biblical perspective on friendships and relationships in general. YHWH alone creates, saves, and makes one whole. Beloved friends are one of YHWH's many gifts to us. What a considerate, ever-loving, graceful, and merciful God!

Akroartes and Poietes: Are you a hearer and doer of the Word? What are the evidences of your faith? Have you been a faithful friend to fellow brethren? What are your strengths and weaknesses? Study Hebrews 11 and write a biblical definition of faith. Once written, thank YHWH in prayer for the gift of faith and sing to Him, "Great Is Thy Faithfulness."

DAY 4
A FRIEND THAT INFLUENCES (1 SAMUEL 14:7)

The ability to influence is seen as a virtue in the world. Influence changes lives and results in some type of growth or shift in lifestyle. How one influences—that is to say, the nature of what one imparts to another human being—differs dramatically between celebrity, country, and culture. The world says it is good to influence people so to focus on either yourself (selfishly) or to emulate others who are more successful (again, selfishly). Worldly influence seeks to have agendas, ideologies, or philosophies imparted so to have others unified in mind, regardless of its emotional, moral, or spiritual value. Influencing according to the world, consciously and unconsciously, exalts and glorifies the will of *humanity alone*.

This is not the will of YHWH. He desires to be glorified *alone*. He desires His "will be done, on earth as it is in heaven" (Matthew 6:10). He desires for influence to come not from worldly individuals or institutions, but rather from His "holy nation" of believers, past and present (1 Peter 2:9), shining as a light to the unbelieving nations. He desires Messiah-centredness and that the brethren influence one another to emulate the One that raised them from spiritual death (cf. 1 Corinthians 11:1). Godly influence, focusing on Him and His commandments, is the only type of influence a believer should seek out, or seek to share, with those around them.

Jonathan was such a believer, and that made him a desirable friend. When facing odds that naturally seemed impossible, he believed that YHWH was capable of anything. Jonathan knew that if YHWH had been faithful to His people in the past, He would be faithful again in

A Friend That Influences (1 Samuel 14:7)

the future. This mindset and trait were not only recognised by Jonathan's armour bearer, it was emulated by him. Godly character in one individual influenced another individual to cultivate godly character. Eternal life in YHWH eclipsed possible temporal death by the Philistine. Speaking to Jonathan, that armour bearer declared in 1 Samuel 14:7 to do "all that is in your heart; turn yourself, and here I am with you according to your desire." Jonathan's influence on this man was so profound that he was ready to tread the same path of sanctification, following in Jonathan's footsteps, which ultimately led to YHWH's divine will. Jonathan was faithful to YHWH, and that influenced those around him.

Jonathan's ability to influence those in his midst in a godly manner would have caused David to recognize that Jonathan was a friend who not only had a positive impact on himself but also on those around them. David would have seen a consistency in public and private circles, an influence in his presence and in his absence. As a friend, we must realise that we will influence those around us by our actions and words. If this is true, then a believer should want to make sure that his influence is godly, good, and full of righteousness. If you are going to influence another, be sure your character is worth emulating. David was all too aware of the importance of reputation, something he would have taught his son Solomon to cultivate (cf. 1 Kings 10:1). A friendship with Jonathan was a safe one because Jonathan's influence on those around him was such that they did not look at Jonathan's works but rather on the works of YHWH through him.

Akroartes and Poietes: Who has influenced you in your walk of faith? How have you influenced others? If you were to assess yourself, would you say you have influenced others negatively or positively?

A Friend That influences (1 Samuel 14:7)

Honestly ask a friend how they see your influence. Ask them where you can improve.

DAY 5

A FRIEND THAT IS WILLING TO GET THEIR HANDS DIRTY
(1 SAMUEL 14:13)

Those that lead by example, who are willing to do the very same task they delegate or instruct others to do, are the type of people we should admire. Those that are willing to get their hands dirty, so-to-speak, and who are willing to break a sweat undergoing even the most menial of tasks, are the type of people we should want to befriend. They appreciate hard work and can never be accused of avoiding work or not willing to practise what they ask of others. They emulate the Messiah.

Jonathan was such an individual. In 1 Samuel 14:13, we read, "Then Jonathan climbed up on his hands and feet, with his armor bearer behind him; and they fell before Jonathan, and his armor bearer put some to death after him." Continuing on from the previous devotion, Jonathan's armour bearer was so influenced by the character of his master that he was willing to follow him into battle. What is notable here is that Jonathan was willing to "climb[…] up on his hands and feet" in order to get where he wanted to be. He did not expect to be carried or have his armour bearer clear the way. He was willing to get dirty. His intention was not necessarily to take the hard route, but the most efficient route. Sometimes, to be conformed means to evade the convenient.

There are a handful of commentators who believe this phrase is used in a negative context, so as to state that a person is willing to forfeit their morals in order to reach a goal. This is clearly not intended here. The phrase can also mean one who is willing to do hard labour because they do not think of themselves as better than the people around them (particularly those that they work for, work over, or work with). They are willing to put effort into their work duties. If that means they will be as dirty and exhausted as those who work for them, so be it. It is better to lead by example and exemplify a willingness to work no matter the expectation or position, than to be seen as too proud to do such tasks. Strong oak trees need dirt to grow.

In a modern context, the concept of humility is frequently overlooked or not emphasized when the topic of leadership is brought up. However, in ancient times, this quality was highly valued. History can often depict leaders as harsh and overbearing in the way they led their people, but in the Scriptures, we see the characteristic of humility as a prized and welcomed model of leadership. To be humble is to know one's place before YHWH. It empties one's self of selfishness and cultivates selflessness. Here is how Mack & Mack define humility:

> [Humility is] an attitude wherein we recognize our own insignificance and unworthiness before YHWH and attribute to Him the supreme honor, praise, prerogatives, rights, privileges, worship, devotion, authority, submission and obedience that He alone deserves. It also involves a natural, habitual tendency to think and behave in a manner that appropriately expresses this attitude. In other words, the attitude of humility is always seen in humble actions. It means having a servant's mind-set and always putting self last.[1]

---

1   Wayne Mack and Joshua Mack. *Humility: The Forgotten Virtue* (Phillipsburg, NJ, P & R Publishing Company, 2005), 26.

A Friend That is Willing to Get Their Hands Dirty (1 Samuel 14:13)

Some may perceive humility as humiliation, and this perspective is likely to be shared by those who observe individuals practicing godly leadership. Yet a humble heart is upheld throughout the Scriptures, starting with the prophets of old, culminating in the life of Yeshua the Messiah, and seen in the legacy of the disciples and beyond. In the earlier books of Scripture, we see the lives of men such as Joseph, Moses, Nathan, and even David, who, despite their flaws, understood the value of living humbly. Humility, then, points upwards to YHWH rather than inwards to self. It considers others more important than one's self.

Akroartes and Poietes: Do you work as hard as those you expect to work for you? Are you humble in spirit? Commit to doing a monthly task that is typically outside your usual purview for a friend in need.

DAY 6

A FRIEND SEES THE DANGER OF SHORT-SIGHTED OATHS (1 SAMUEL 14:29)

In 1 Samuel 14:24-28, we come to a section in which King Saul makes a foolish oath:

> Now the men of Israel were hard-pressed on that day, for Saul had put the people under oath, saying, "Cursed be the man who eats food before evening, and until I have avenged myself on my enemies." So none of the people tasted food. All the people of the land entered the forest, and there was honey on the ground. When the people entered the forest, behold, there was a flow of honey; but no man put his hand to his mouth, for the people feared the oath. But Jonathan had not heard when his father put the people under oath; therefore, he put out the end of the staff that was in his hand and dipped it in the honeycomb, and put his hand to his mouth, and his eyes brightened. Then one of the people said, "Your father strictly put the people under oath, saying, 'Cursed be the man who eats food today.'" And the people were weary.
> —1 Samuel 14:24-28

In hearing this, Jonathan responded wisely, as one who could see the "big picture." He saw the danger of short-sighted oaths. He replied in 1 Samuel 14:29-30 as follows:

A Friend Sees the Danger of Short-Sighted Oaths (1 Samuel 14:29)

> My father has troubled the land. See now, how my eyes have brightened because I tasted a little of this honey. How much more, if only the people had eaten freely today of the spoil of their enemies which they found! For now the slaughter among the Philistines has not been great.
>
> —1 Samuel 14:29-30

Jonathan was the type of person who assessed what was in front of him as much as what was around him. He thought about the small things as well as the large things. He could see how life's moments connected to one another, and he understood that all actions have consequences, whether good and bad. He worked towards seeing life's circumstances from the perspective of YHWH.

This was the type of friend David desired and received in Jonathan. In turn, he was the same type of friend to Jonathan. While this is not to say that the men didn't have flaws or sins, for they certainly did, they were men who understood their place in the big scheme of things and understood that they were a small part in YHWH's plan for Israel.

Jonathan and David saw the "big picture" of their actions and the dangers of short-sighted oaths, unlike King Saul. Having such a friend ensures that one is not careless when making oaths. We live in a time when many people make careless oaths—some more costly than others—to the point that oaths have lost their original meaning and value. Oaths are often either made without any genuine intention of fulfillment or are so infused with emotion that they verge on becoming a farce. Oaths were once intended to be imbued with meaning for those who spoke it and those who heard it. They were a verbal contract that was an extension of one's character, and to break it was to wound one's character. Short-sighted oaths were not a characteristic a friend

A Friend Sees the Danger of Short-Sighted Oaths (1 Samuel 14:29)

should be known for. If you were going to make an oath, it was to be done with integrity.

Today, oaths are unnecessary, but the notion of being careful with your words and seeing the big picture of your actions and words remains. Common sense is desirable in a friendship. And do not be fooled: *common sense is not as common as you might think it is.*

Akroartes and Poietes: Are you short-sighted, or do you see the "big picture"? List some examples in which you failed in the first and succeeded in the second. Pray to YHWH and ask Him for forgiveness for any careless oaths you have made. If you have done the same to family or friends, apologise to them, and rectify the situation as much as possible.

DAY 7

A FRIEND IS WILLING TO ACCEPT CONSEQUENCES (1 SAMUEL 14:43)

In the wake of Jonathan breaking his father's oath, we read in 1 Samuel 14:43 that "Saul said to Jonathan, 'Tell me what you have done.' So, Jonathan told him and said, 'I indeed tasted a little honey with the end of the staff that was in my hand. Here I am, I must die!'" Jonathan was right in the sense that he saw the "big picture" and danger of short-sighted oaths. However, he was wrong in that he was not honouring his father by his attitude. As such, he laid his very life before his father and was willing to accept the consequences for his disobedience, even if it meant his death. As beautifully sweet as honey is, there remained in his mouth the bitterness of not honouring his parent as commanded by YHWH.

A biblical friend is someone who is willing to admit their wrongdoing and accept the consequences. They do not avoid, flee, or deceive when it comes to facing the consequences of their actions. They embrace the responsibility that comes with their role and its duties. And even if the world deems their actions and words acceptable, if they do not align with the Scriptures, the believer will ensure that justice and righteousness as defined by YHWH are upheld. They do not conform to the world and love its ways; they are Kingdom-minded and seek to glorify YHWH.

It is extremely tempting to justify Jonathan's actions, for, as the world says, the ends justify the means. Biblically speaking, this is erroneous (cf. Romans 12:21). Believers must not seek a conclusion or goal that bypasses biblical alignment and integrity. Jonathan was

A Friend is Willing to Accept Consequences (1 Samuel 14:43)

aware of the commandments of YHWH, the means of sanctification for those separated from the nations as the Assembly of YHWH. Yet, he broke Exodus 20:12. He did not honour his father, even though his oath was foolish. Death awaited him not because he broke the commandment of YHWH, but because of his father's vow. Thankfully, Saul did not follow through with his threat, but this story reveals the strong character of Jonathan. It reveals that he was a man, a son, a best friend, who was willing to accept the consequences of his actions.

This quality in friendship is rare. Not only did Jonathan exhibit it, but so did David. In the wake of committing adultery with Bathsheba, the child she birthed from that sinful encounter was struck sick by the Lord and would soon thereafter pass away:

> David therefore inquired of God for the child; and David fasted and went and lay all night on the ground. The elders of his household stood beside him in order to raise him up from the ground, but he was unwilling and would not eat food with them. Then it happened on the seventh day that the child died. And the servants of David were afraid to tell him that the child was dead, for they said, "Behold, while the child was still alive, we spoke to him and he did not listen to our voice. How then can we tell him that the child is dead, since he might do himself harm!" But when David saw that his servants were whispering together, David perceived that the child was dead; so David said to his servants, "Is the child dead?" And they said, "He is dead." So David arose from the ground, washed, anointed himself, and changed his clothes; and he came into the house of the Lord and worshiped. Then he came to his own house, and when he requested, they set food before him and he ate. Then his servants said to him,

A Friend is Willing to Accept Consequences (1 Samuel 14:43)

"What is this thing that you have done? While the child was alive, you fasted and wept; but when the child died, you arose and ate food." He said, "While the child was still alive, I fasted and wept; for I said, 'Who knows, the Lord may be gracious to me, that the child may live.' But now he has died; why should I fast? Can I bring him back again?
—2 Samuel 12:15-23

David swiftly accepted the consequences of his actions, so much so that the elders of Israel were unsettled. They even feared he would take his own life over it, yet David refrained and knew he had sinned against YHWH and others by his adultery. His conviction conformed him.

Akroartes and Poietes: Are you willing to accept the consequences for your actions? Consider examples. Are there consequences to sin you have avoided? Seek biblical forgiveness and restoration.

DAY 8

A FRIEND WORKS WITH YHWH (1 SAMUEL 14:45)

In the previous devotion, I mentioned that Saul did not kill Jonathan for his obedience. But to be clear, that was not because he didn't want to. In fact, he was more than willing to take the life of his son. His sword did not discriminate. Saul had not made a biblical vow (Numbers 30:1-2), but rather, proclaimed a curse by his oath. Jonathan not abiding by his father's oath would not incur the wrath of YHWH, for he had not broken a commandment of the Law. However, Saul, as king of Israel, did not want to come across as weak or as showing favouritism because Jonathan was his son. So, in his mind, Jonathan had to die in order to serve as an example to any in the nation who would seek to defy their king.

In 1 Samuel 14:45, we read that the nation as a whole was not at all happy with this:

> But the people said to Saul, "Must Jonathan die, who has brought about this great deliverance in Israel? Far from it! As the Lord lives, not one hair of his head shall fall to the ground, for he has worked with God this day."
> —1 Samuel 14:45

In the next devotion, we will explore how the people deeply respected Jonathan, but today we will focus on the phrase that Jonathan "worked with YHWH."

Jonathan worked with YHWH in that his actions defeated the Philistines, the sworn enemies of YHWH. Prior to Saul, they had caused tribulation in the lives of Samson (Judges 13:1; 14:1) and the prophet Samuel (1 Samuel 4:1). 1 Samuel 14:6 makes clear that Jonathan believed YHWH was with him in his military campaign, and this declaration must have been shared unto the people by his armour bearer. The people believed that Jonathan was a man who served YHWH first, and while Jonathan loved and served his king and earthly father, his Heavenly Father and King was his foremost love. Jonathan had not broken a commandment by disobeying his father's human oath, but Saul's self-made rules meant that his son could have been killed for breaking his oath. As I proposed in the previous devotion, the closest Jonathan came to sinning (and not to the point of deserving capital punishment) is that he was not the most honourable in his response to his father's oath when he broke it, foolish as it was. Now, had this been the first of several instances in which Jonathan rebelled and even cursed his father, he would have gone on to break one of the actual commandments of YHWH, and it would have been acceptable for him to have been publicly executed in the wake of Saul bringing his case to the elders of the nation (cf. Deuteronomy 21:18–21). He did not, however, and it is a fair statement to make that, despite Saul's many flaws as a father and leader, Jonathan was more often than not honourable towards his father.

Jonathan's commitment to YHWH and his willingness to work with YHWH, who is providential and sovereign in His rule, is a hallmark of biblical friendship. It is a heart that loves YHWH with every fibre ("hair" even!) of their being and is attentive to the Word and will of the One who inspired its every book. Jonathan respected human authority, but he respected YHWH more and understood that sometimes those in power—whatever type of authority or government it is—can and will overstep their boundaries. At the end of the day, we

A Friend Works With YHWH (1 Samuel 14:45)

must instinctively walk alongside YHWH when human rationale is eclipsed by the divine.

This is the type of friend you want to be and have alongside you, when working with YHWH.

Akroartes and Poietes: Do you see your life as both serving and working for YHWH? Do you prioritise YHWH above your leaders and management? Take an inventory of how you work for YHWH, and speak with the male elders at your local assembly to discuss how you can explore and strengthen ways to work for YHWH in and outside the local assembly.

DAY 9
A FRIEND IS RESPECTED BY OTHERS (1 SAMUEL 14:45)

> But the people said to Saul, "Must Jonathan die, who has brought about this great deliverance in Israel? Far from it! As the Lord lives, not one hair of his head shall fall to the ground, for he has worked with God this day." *So the people rescued Jonathan and he did not die.*
> —1 Samuel 14:45; emphasis added

As we discussed in the previous devotion, this was the response of the people when they were told that Jonathan would face capital punishment by his father because he disobeyed him and broke an oath. We highlighted that Jonathan was a man and friend that "worked with YHWH." Today, we will look at how Jonathan is respected by others.

Imagine, in the wake of a confession deserving of punishment, a crowd emerged to defend you—a crowd so large and unanimous in their belief that you should be free that the human individual intending on punishing you refrained and embraced the will of the people. Imagine a leader who is so moved by the love and respect of the community as a whole that he is not able to follow through with what he initially perceived as an injustice. This is what happened with Jonathan. Jonathan's character and reputation preceded himself. He was a man of integrity, one who sought to do what was good according to YHWH. He was not perfect, but he was humble and sought grace, love, and peace over separation from YHWH and others. The people could see the heart of Jonathan; it was a heart that worked with YHWH, a heart after YHWH's heart (cf. 1 Samuel 13:14). This resulted in a respect

A Friend is Respected by Others (1 Samuel 14:45)

from the people of the nation, believer and unbeliever alike. We are not told that those amassed here were just believers, so we can safely assume that this group represented the people as a whole and included the godly remnant and those who were not.

To be a friend respected by all people, whether they believe in YHWH or not, is quite an impressive characteristic. It is not a case of pandering to the world; it is walking in such a manner to ensure others find no fault in who you are. History and perhaps your own life attests to those who, while unsaved, see the kindness, love, and value of the Christian faith. It is interesting to note that a man called to be an elder in the local assembly "must have a good reputation with those outside the local assembly, so that he will not fall into reproach and the snare of the devil" (1 Timothy 3:7). Truth be told, all believers, not just elders, should exhibit this.

We live in a world today where respect is not desirable or practised as it once was. In being respectable, more often than not, a person receives respect. Being respected by those around you, because you are consistent and unhypocritical, is something we should all strive for. Jonathan was such a man, and so was David. He respected Saul, even though Saul wanted him killed (1 Samuel 24:10), and even mourned over him when he passed away (2 Samuel 1:17). Respect can be given even after death.

A friend is respected by others. In being respected by others, they can be trusted to do what is right and can be trusted to be the same person in private as they are in public. If deemed necessary by the Lord, they will have those people around them come to their aid because of their reputation. Living in a Godly manner before all people, whether they are saved or not, ensures that you avoid reproach and demonic snares. Moreover, when you face oppression or persecution, you can

A Friend is Respected by Others (1 Samuel 14:45)

rely on YHWH, who is your "avenger who brings wrath on the one who practices evil" (Romans 13:4).

Akroartes and Poietes: Are you respected by those in and outside the local assembly? Reach out instinctively to seek support or encouragement from someone within your local congregation whom you may not know well, as well as from an unbelieving neighbour. Do not consider this a one off, but the beginning of a godly pattern in your life and for your maturing character.

DAY 10

A FRIEND ACKNOWLEDGES THAT FRIENDS HAVE OTHER FRIENDS
(1 KINGS 5:1, 7)

The great thing about friends is that you can have more than one. In fact, as someone within the Body of Messiah (Ephesians 4:12; 1 Corinthians 12:27), it will only be natural that you will have more than one friend. It is also great how each friend can differ in their strengths and how they relate to you. There are some friendship groups in which everyone gets along, and there are friendship groups in which each friendship revolves around a sole individual.

You might find it surprising that Jonathan wasn't David's only intimate friend, and it's likely that he not only accepted that but also encouraged the diversity within David's circle of friends. The other close friend of David was Hiram, king of Tyre. In 2 Samuel 5:11, we read that Hiram loved David so much that he "sent messengers to David with cedar trees and carpenters and stonemasons; and... built a house for David." We know that they had a covenantal relationship, as 1 Kings 5:1 says that he "sent his servants to Solomon, when he heard that they had anointed him king in place of his father, *for Hiram had always been a friend of David*" (emphasis added). The Hebrew word for "always," *kôl,* speaks of totality and wholeness. Hiram praised David when he found out he had a son, declaring in 1 Kings 5:7, "Blessed be the Lord today, who has given to David a wise son over this great people." This friendship must have had a depth of intimacy so great, that it extended unto his son Solomon in his later years. As he had given David resources, Hiram gave Solomon resources (1 Kings 5:8,

10). As he had peace and covenantal love with David, Hiram cultivated the same with Solomon (1 Kings 5:12). What was Hiram's, was the house of David's (cf. 1 Kings 9:14, 27; 10:11, 22).

Hiram "had always been a friend of David." This speaks of lived history. It speaks of experiences shared. It speaks of time alone and with extended family. Some commentators suggest Hiram was a pagan believer, being a Gentile from Tyre, yet I contend that his prayer to YHWH (1 Kings 5:7) and involvement in building the Temple with Solomon suggest otherwise. It is clear that, alongside Jonathan, Hiram was a good friend of David's. Both Hiram and Jonathan would have known about one another, yet neither was threatened by their shared friendship with David. Each contributed and drew something different from the king. Soon after hearing of Hiram for the last time in Scripture (1 Kings 10:22), Solomon "turned away from the Lord" (1 Kings 11:9). I am speculating here, but I wonder if Hiram passed away soon after, and that without encouraging and likeminded friends (and remembering how his father reacted in the wake of Jonathan's death), King Solomon's moral and spiritual compass failed. If so, his example should warn us not to take our friendships for granted and to practise what we learn from them, whether our friends are in our presence or they are in Heaven.

A biblical friend acknowledges their friend has other friends, *and that is both good and should be encouraged*. This is not a competition. There is no self in community. Encourage the growth of friendships, for one can never have too many.

Akroartes and Poietes: Reflect on the diversity of friends you have had, past and present. Where do they differ, and how have each uniquely challenged and complemented you and your walk of faith? Be intentional, physically at the local assembly and spiritually in prayer,

A Friend Acknowledges That Friends Have Other Friends (1 Kings 5:1, 7)

in establishing new friendships. Avoid merely gravitating towards individuals with similar personalities and shared interests; instead, actively seek out diverse friendships that have the potential to foster personal and spiritual growth in your walk with YHWH.

DAY 11

A FRIEND KNITS THEIR SOUL TO THEIR FRIEND'S SOUL
(1 SAMUEL 18:1)

It is one of the most beautiful phrases in Scripture: "Now it came about when he had finished speaking to Saul, that *the soul of Jonathan was knit to the soul of David*, and Jonathan loved him as himself" (1 Samuel 18:1; emphasis added). The Hebrew word here for "knit," *qâshar*, speaks of being bound or joined together. In Proverbs 6:21, Solomon told his children that regarding the commandments of parents, a child must "[*qâshar*] them continually on your heart." It is not indestructible, but intimate. It is not a given, but must be intentional.

I use this phrase often when speaking of what a biblical friendship is and should be. The word friend is so carelessly used today, yet should be ripe with meaning. To befriend an individual and invest in them should be led by a desire to knit into one another. In order to make a piece of clothing or a rug reliable and strong, one must knit continually and deeply so that it holds and becomes what it is intended to be. No one throws balls of wool together and expects them to become something useful. Knitting takes time. It takes patience. One of the fruits of the Holy Spirit is patience (Galatians 5:22). Essentially, it is *holy waiting*. By waiting for YHWH (who is holy) you are being sanctified (the process of becoming holy). The more you knit, the stronger the piece you are working on, and the image of what you set out to achieve begins to form. Likewise, the more you knit the souls of two friends, the stronger the piece you are working on, and the image of unity the Scriptures speak of begins to take form.

Knitting, as I mentioned earlier, is intentional. From the knitting needle and the type of yarn to the stich type and style of weaving, it all requires a conscious effort, structured time, and ongoing commitment. Friendships are no different. Jonathan's and David's souls were not knit in a day, week, month, or even a year. Their bond was formed beyond the constraints of time, meaning there was no predetermined number of seconds; instead, it was nurtured with a mindset that cultivates a friendship naturally. If you are not willing to invest in a friendship, to weave them into the fabric of your life, then why call them a friend?

The apostle Paul used this same concept in Colossians 2:1-3 when he wrote, "I want you to know how great a struggle I have on your behalf and for those who are at Laodicea, and for all those who have not personally seen my face, that their hearts may be encouraged, having been knit together in love, and attaining to all the wealth that comes from the full assurance of understanding, resulting in a true knowledge of God's mystery, that is, Christ Himself, in whom are hidden all the treasures of wisdom and knowledge." The word used for "knit," *symbibázō*, speaks of being affectionately joined together and having the same mind. The deep connection shared by Jonathan and David was something that Paul aspired to replicate within his own circle of friends. We, too, should desire to be knit to the soul of another who feels the same as we do.

Akroartes and Poietes: Do you desire to have the type of intimate friendship that David and Jonathan had? What barriers and fears do you have when embarking on the quest to find such a friend or when striving to become such a friend? Commit to pray for the desire to establish new friends and to become a friend like Nathan. Do not be afraid or resistant to talk to other brethren about what a friendship looks like.

DAY 12

A FRIEND LOVES THEIR FRIEND AS THEY LOVE THEMSELVES (1 SAMUEL 18:2)

As a believer who read and studied the Scriptures, Jonathan would have memorized Deuteronomy 6:5: "You shall love the Lord your God with all your heart and with all your soul and with all your might." He also would have known Leviticus 19:18: "You shall not take vengeance, nor bear any grudge against the sons of your people, but you shall love your neighbor as yourself; I am the Lord." These were the greatest commandments according to our Messiah, Yeshua, as they summarised (not nullified) the entire Law (Mark 12:28-31). They encapsulated a love in thought, word, and deed. Know God, know others, and make Him known.

Jonathan was a friend who loved others as he loved himself. His actions were loving. King Saul recognised that the "soul of Jonathan was knit to the soul of David" (1 Samuel 18:1), and as such, integrated him into his household (1 Samuel 18:2). This allowed Jonathan to practise the love he had for his friend and cultivate their friendship in a way distance rarely allows for something to develop in full.

As I mentioned in the first devotion, there have been progressively liberal "Christians" who have sought to rationalise homosexuality by appealing to the friendship of Jonathan and David. Their argument is based on the assumption that David and Jonathan's intimate friendship must have included romantic love akin to that between a husband and wife. They use this assumption to justify their sins, sometimes even dismissing or attempting to reinterpret the commandments against such abominable practises by attributing them to cultural and historical contexts. This line of reasoning then extends to asserting that if homosexuality was deemed acceptable in the past, it should also be considered acceptable today. This is a lie and abuse of Scripture. The love shared by Jonathan and David, a love where they cared for each other as they cared for themselves, represents the high standard of love to which all brethren are called (cf. Matthew 22:37-40). They practised what the Scriptures preached. They provided an example for us to emulate.

Homosexuality is a sin. Whether between men or between women, YHWH has made it clear throughout his entire revealed Word that those who practise this sinful lifestyle will not enter the Kingdom of Heaven, as they have substituted Yeshua for their sexual lust. The apostle Paul, inspired by the Holy Spirit, makes clear: "do you not know that the unrighteous will not inherit the kingdom of YHWH? Do not be deceived; neither fornicators, nor idolaters, nor adulterers, nor effeminate, nor homosexuals, nor thieves, nor the covetous, nor drunkards, nor revilers, nor swindlers, will inherit the kingdom of God" (1 Corinthians 6:8-10). YHWH does not tolerate any forms of sexual perversion. In this context, the sinners are not those who are tempted by or wrestling with these feelings in their faith journey. Paul is addressing those who have fully embraced these behaviors, rationalized them, and who believe it's acceptable to be a believer while continuing to engage in their beloved sins. It is a wilful choice, one that no longer sees sin as sin. It is, however, deceptive and hellish.

Jonathan loved David; David loved Jonathan. We should love our friend in such a way. We should love them not merely with our minds and emotions, but also with our words and actions. Our love for brethren should be so real, that if they needed to live with us or be looked after by us for a season, it should come naturally to us. This love was

A Friend Loves Their Friend as They Love Themselves (1 Samuel 18:2)

demonstrated amongst the first believers in Messiah Yeshua (Acts 2:44-47). It is the same love we are called to today.

Akroartes and Poietes: Do you love your friends as yourself? How so? If not, where are you struggling to do so? Is it a sinful reason, or are you able to overcome it with the Lord? Also, do you know someone struggling with or enslaved to homosexuality? Have you shared the gospel with them? Today, love your friend as yourself by doing or saying something good to them. And ensure that you do this regularly, without prompting and in hope of it becoming natural to you. Also, pray for someone you know who is homosexual, and if possible, show them the love of Yeshua while also sharing with them the truth. Teach them that they can have a sanctified friendship in Messiah and that you can help them in that walk, if they repent and declare Him as their Lord and Saviour.

DAY 13
A FRIEND IS COVENANTAL IN THEIR VIEW OF FRIENDSHIP (1 SAMUEL 18:3)

A defining moment in the friendship between Jonathan and David occurred when Jonathan entered into a covenant with David. In 1 Samuel 18:3, we read that "Jonathan made a covenant with David because he loved him as himself." This was a different love than that of the forthcoming promise to David of Saul's daughter as a wife (cf. 1 Samuel 17:25). It was brotherly love.

In the Bible, the word covenant means "to cut" (cf. Genesis 15) and refers to a formal agreement. These covenants can be either conditional or unconditional and were frequently made between YHWH and an individual or between two or more individuals (i.e., alliances). A covenant could be established for a designated period of time or indefinitely, and at times (but not always) involved a ritual to seal it. All divine-instituted covenants of YHWH are still operative and relevant to the believer today.

The covenant in 1 Samuel 18:3, then, is between human individuals. We are not given much information as to the nature of the covenant, though. Whether it was conditional or unconditional is unclear, but it was meant to exist beyond their earthly lives, as attested by David's reference to it at Jonathan's wake (2 Samuel 1:36) and in his blessing of Jonathan's son with the formerly owned lands of Saul (2 Samuel 21:7). It was also different from the Davidic Covenant ordained by YHWH (2 Samuel 7:10-13).

We cannot be certain how early David came to know about the Davidic Covenant, but moments like this would prepare him for the gravity of larger moments like that which was promised to him by YHWH. The "Davidic Covenant" (2 Samuel 7:10-13; 1 Chronicles 17:11-14; 2 Chronicles 6:16; Psalm 89:25-35) was the unconditional promise of YHWH that from the House of David (that is to say, the YHWH-sanctioned earthly kingdom that King David built and established his earthly lineage), the prophesised Messiah will arise ("descendant" or "seed"; cf. 2 Samuel 7:12). It is a national covenant, which would be prepared through the marriage and birth of selected individuals, until the designated time in which the Messiah would be born (cf. Matthew 1; Luke 3:23-38). YHWH promised that the Messiah would come through David's house, but also, that his house would be established forever, eternal in nature (2 Samuel 7:16; 1 Chronicles 17:14; Psalm 89:29); it will be completely fulfilled and witnessed in the future and literal Millennium (Revelation 20:2-7; cf. Isaiah 9:3–7; 11:1–10), after the Messiah's second coming. It is no surprise that the covenant was with King David as opposed to King Saul before him, as David was the intended choice of YHWH for Israel's kingdom.

Jonathan's covenant with David is something that is missing from many friendships today. To think covenantally about friendships, and to live out friendships with that mindset, would both deepen and strengthen our appreciation of what a biblical friendship should be.

Akroartes and Poietes: Do you think about friendships covenantally? For you are married, do you think of your marriage covenantally? If not, consider how you can seek to rectify this. Study the Scriptures and document those covenants made between humans. If you were to create a covenant between you and your friend, what would it look like? If you are able, draft a covenant, finalise it and commit it to prayer.

DAY 14

A FRIEND SHARES RESOURCES WITH THEIR FRIEND (1 SAMUEL 18:4)

There is an old saying: "What's yours is mine and what's mine is yours." This can be understood in a positive way. Jonathan was a friend who was willing to share that which he owned with his friend, David. Some commentators speculate whether 1 Samuel 18:4 is Jonathan symbolically handing over succession to David (foreshadowing his kingship) or possibly military succession (in the wake of Saul's actions in v. 5). Either—even both—are possible interpretations, but we can see here *an act of friendship*. In the wake of their covenantal love being established in the verse before, Jonathan shares some of his most important possessions. He does not flinch in seeing that if one truly loves another as they love themselves, then they are able to share beyond what is seen as "normal" in the world (cf. 1 Samuel 18:2).

When friends are integrated into families and their households, where are the boundaries? What are *your* boundaries? What are you willing to provide and share with them? How much time are you willing to share with them? How much food and drink are you willing to share? Are you holding onto clothes, money, and other belongings with a clenched fist, or are you able to let go of them?

This is not some form of communism, but communitarianism. There is a distinct difference—a fundamental difference, in fact. The former is coerced and sanctioned distribution of resources, whereas the latter is personal and voluntary sharing of resources. However, one must be sure to make clear the ideological foundation of communitarianism, for in reality, only one is acceptable to the believer: that which is founded on the Scriptures. The reason and source of community is YHWH: God the Father, Son, and Spirit. The Body of Messiah is communal in nature; it is diverse smaller communities (the local assembly) that make up a unified larger community (the universal Assembly). We as believers are involved in several communities, and each are often connected to the other because of their fellowship in Messiah: marriage, immediate family, extended family, friends, local assembly, ministry groups, the universal assembly, and several others.

Jonathan shared what he had with David because he loved him, a love of knitted souls and covenantal depth. Even if we were to interpret this verse as symbolically handing over succession, Jonathan was a man that believed that *every* resource he had *was from YHWH*. What is brought into this world and held onto cannot be taken into the afterlife. As such, who is to say that what YHWH has given His children could not be used in different ways and for more than one person? Again, this is not to say that right now, we should give everything away to those people we love, but rather, we should be open and willing to share what we have if the need arises—and at times, simply because we want to bless another. I still have the receipt that preserves the moment when a brother in Messiah bought me an expensive piece of hardware that I needed! I saved it, as it as symbol of a selfless act in our friendship, of blessing a friend simply for the joy that it brings. In establishing a covenant with David, Jonathan naturally believed that they shared all things as a community would. In doing so, Jonathan gives us a model of friendship that is a picture of what godly community should be. Another old saying "blood is thicker than water," which esteems family above everything, is biblically inaccurate (cf. Matthew 12:46-50). While earthly families of blood are close, temporal, and worthy of love, spiritual families of the shed blood of Messiah are eternal, and we

A Friend Shares Resources With Their Friend (1 Samuel 18:4)

are meant to love them *in an even deeper way*. Jonathan loved his unbelieving father and sisters, but loved believers like David even more.

Akroartes and Poietes: What do you currently share with your friends? How much do you share? What are you unwilling to share or have not considered sharing with them? How do you feel about sharing in general? Do you see all that you have and own as coming from YHWH and as His possession? Seek out something that a friend needs at the moment. Commit it to prayer and see if you are able to accommodate or bless them where they are in need.

DAY 15

A FRIEND DELIGHTS IN THEIR FRIEND
(1 SAMUEL 19:1)

Displeased with the ascension of David and his friendship with Jonathan, Saul "told Jonathan his son and all his servants to put David to death. But Jonathan, Saul's son, greatly delighted in David" (1 Samuel 19:1). Jonathan was not one that shared the hatred of his father. He saw in David something he had not found in others, an authenticity of character and devotion to YHWH that had been absent from his own household.

The word "delight" in Hebrew, *châphêts*, speaks of an inclination and pleasure towards that which is desirable or favourable, and is used throughout the Scriptures to depict intimacy between or from YHWH (1 Kings 10:9; Psalm 40:8; Isaiah 53:10), individuals (Genesis 34:19; Esther 2:14), and even the Scriptures themselves (Psalm 112:1). It speaks of a disposition towards the object of affection and does not shift with peripheral changes or circumstances. It speaks of joyful fire rather than the fleeting happiness, hence the difference between the two; the former is temporary, sometimes shallow, and worldly, while the latter is eternal, deep, and godly (Psalm 51:11-12; Romans 15:13; Galatians 5:22; 1 Thessalonians 1:6).

Jonathan delighted in David. David delighted in Jonathan. A believer can express delight towards another in a myriad of ways. They can delight in the way they think about them. Their thoughts are positive and warm, considerate of how their beloved friend is walking with the Lord, how their marriage or relationships are, whether they are embarking on new friendships and other such matters. They can delight in the way that they speak of their friend. This will be explored more in the next devotion, but to speak of one's friends in a consistent and edifying way reveals the delight they have towards them. To speak of them in an uplifting manner, intentionally highlighting their goodness as defined by YHWH. Finally, they can delight in their friend by their actions, the deeds they do for them or inspired by them. To emulate them because of their close walk with the Lord and manifestation of the commandments of YHWH, a friend can delight in their friend by learning from them and following the same steps as theirs in Messiah.

Personally speaking, I once had a friend that I loved as a brother. A man of authenticity and integrity, a brother in Messiah who has gone through many personal trials and tribulations. He left school early, secured a vocation as a mechanic, yet was called by YHWH to leave that highly paid profession to take up school chaplaincy. Though his income was halved overnight, he trusted in YHWH and after several years, in the absence of any qualifications other than life experience, became the head chaplain within the company. It was inspiring how he handled himself as a husband and father of nine, among believers and even unbelievers, and those who constantly tried to undermine him. He is one of the few men that inspired me in life and cultivated in me the desire to be a better man in Messiah. He led by example, was selfless, and expected nothing in return for helping others. He used to contact me regularly to see how I was and how my walk in Messiah was without any prompting. He made himself available regardless of the time of day. He served with the heart of a deacon and was worthy of mirroring.

What Jonathan and David had is what my friend and I had. Before I was married, he modelled to me what a husband and father should be. Today, I have another admirable brother in my life, whom I dedicated this devotional to, and whom I respect and consider family. My

A Friend Delights in Their Friend (1 Samuel 19:1)

children call him and his wife "uncle" and "aunty," and our families intentionally spend time together. We practise the biblical festivals, and in him I see a man not of perfection, but of authenticity and integrity. We delight in YHWH first and foremost. So, I can delight in him.

His presence in my life has been a blessing and has sharpened me (Proverbs 27:17). Are you the same to your friend, and have they blessed you as a friend?

Akroartes and Poietes: Do you delight in your friend? How would you explain it? Contact at least one friend today and tell them how they have been a blessing to you. If you prefer not to call them directly, send them a text or card expressing this.

DAY 16

A FRIEND SPEAKS WELL OF THEIR FRIEND (1 SAMUEL 19:1)

In response to his father's call to kill David, Jonathan spoke to his friend and then went directly to his father:

> So Jonathan told David saying, "Saul my father is seeking to put you to death. Now therefore, please be on guard in the morning, and stay in a secret place and hide yourself. I will go out and stand beside my father in the field where you are, and I will speak with my father about you; if I find out anything, then I will tell you." *Then Jonathan spoke well of David* to Saul his father and said to him, "Do not let the king sin against his servant David, since he has not sinned against you, and since his deeds have been very beneficial to you. For he took his life in his hand and struck the Philistine, and the Lord brought about a great deliverance for all Israel; you saw it and rejoiced. Why then will you sin against innocent blood by putting David to death without a cause?
> —1 Samuel 19:2-5, emphasis added

Jonathan spoke well of David. He wasn't the kind of friend that would speak of their friends differently based on the situation or the person they were speaking to. He was consistent, and while he did not whitewash David's sins, he focused more on his goodness and achievements before the Lord. Jonathan spoke well of his friend with others and knew that David would do the same in his absence. Jonathan

A Friend Speaks Well of Their Friend (1 Samuel 19:1)

spoke the truth with his father and did not let emotions reign. He did not seek to edit his thoughts or manipulate his father's thinking, but spoke from a biblical heart. He didn't need to bend the truth, lie by admission or omission, or win a debate by using tears or raising his voice. He simply spoke well of David. He could speak nothing else.

We see in this passage the principle of being consistent. Notice that Jonathan spoke to both men with composure and reason, as well as with selflessness and compassion. One man, David, loved him as deeply as he did as a friend, while the second man tolerated him and seemed to hate his beloved friend. Yet, Jonathan was the same man in both environments before both men. This is an important lesson to learn and emulate.

Friends focus on delighting in the holiness of one another, how the Lord is working in them, strengthening them by His Sprit, and conforming them into the image of the Son, Yeshua. Jonathan and David may have not fully understood the Trinitarian nature of YHWH (cf. Psalm 110:1; Matthew 22:44), but what they did know was a saving faith. They knew they were sinners and needed a Saviour (cf. Psalm 51:5). There is no doubt that they encouraged the other in the Lord and to live His commandments. A friend does not delight in their friend by focusing on their sins, their flesh and failings, other than to convict, challenge, and then be comforted in their one whom they love first and foremost, YHWH.

Akroartes and Poietes: How do you speak of your friends? Do you defend their honour when they are spoken of poorly? Are you consistent in your character? Do you know how your friends speak of you? Be intentional this month about speaking well of your friends, whether they come up in conversation or by you introducing them into a conversation.

DAY 17
A FRIEND IS A VOICE OF REASON FOR THEIR FRIEND
(1 SAMUEL 19:6)

In the wake of the passage from the last devotion, in which Jonathan appealed for the life of his friend David, "Saul listened to the voice of Jonathan, and Saul vowed, 'As the Lord lives, he shall not be put to death'" (1 Samuel 19:6). Jonathan's reasoning with his father, stating that he would be sinning against YHWH and David if he had his friend killed, and that David's "deeds have been very beneficial" to Saul and resulted in blessing from the Lord (1 Samuel 19:4-5), resulted in the rational decision of Saul to abstain from enacting the death penalty.

Jonathan's voice of reason for David not only protected his beloved friend, but also saved Saul from the wrath of YHWH. If he had killed David, he would have been accused of shedding innocent blood (Deuteronomy 19:10, 21:8). He would have been charged with bloodguiltiness. The capital punishment he threated upon David would have become a reality to the King of Israel. Jonathan did not delight in seeing others harmed, whether by the hand of irrational men or by their own hands. David would have seen in Jonathan a man of reason, one who was consistent in his love for YHWH and love for others; he did not unbiblically react to dire or problematic scenarios, but rather sought to act in a manner consistent with the Scriptures.

David may have learned from this event, for he avoided repeating the same sin himself (1 Samuel 25:26, 31). This is not to say that there were times in the kingship of David that he was unreasonable, for we have many examples, but cooler heads prevail when one does not act

A Friend is a Voice of Reason for Their Friend (1 Samuel 19:6)

in the storm of emotions. While not advocating for secular psychology in any form or manner, it is amusing to see the secular world "borrow" from the Scriptures and the life of David's son Solomon in creating what is called the "Solomon Paradox." It is the belief that there are some people who are significantly wiser about other people's problems than their own. They are intuitional and perceptive about others, but they are emotionally blind to their own problems. While this may be true for some, David had much to learn from Jonathan. He was wise regarding his actions, in addition to those around him, yet exhibited no pride. Unknowingly, he emulated an attribute of YHWH, who is infinitely reasonable (cf. Isaiah 1:18).

It is without any doubt, though unrecorded, that Jonathan and David would have spoken at great length about many issues and problems, both personal and regarding their roles in the kingdom of Israel. These conversations would have been insightful, for the two would have discussed a plethora of topics and sought conclusions and decisions that were reasonable, consistent with the Scriptures, and reflective of their growing spiritual maturity. While not perfect and bound to sin in their lives, Jonathan's voice of reason for his friend in the face of death itself was a lesson they could return to again and again.

Akroartes and Poietes: Do you confide in your friends, and do they confide in you? Do you seek their counsel when making life decisions after first talking to YHWH, and if married, your spouse? Are both of you a voice of reason in the midst of difficult and emotional events and moments? Commit to ending your evenings with readings from the book of Proverbs. As a work of wisdom, learn and commit to memory its truths so you can share them with friends when they are in need of sound and godly advice.

DAY 18

A FRIEND FINDS FAVOUR IN THEIR FRIEND
(1 SAMUEL 20:3)

David could not understand why Jonathan's father, Saul, wanted him dead. It had become an obsession to the man, one which fluctuated pending on the emotional state of the king of Israel. It caused him much distress, and David was convinced that if given the opportunity, he would lose his life to Saul's blade. We read in 1 Samuel 20:1-3:

> Then David fled from Naioth in Ramah, and came and said to Jonathan, "What have I done? What is my iniquity? And what is my sin before your father, that he is seeking my life?" He said to him, "Far from it, you shall not die. Behold, my father does nothing either great or small without disclosing it to me. So why should my father hide this thing from me? It is not so!" Yet David vowed again, saying, "*Your father knows well that I have found favor in your sight*, and he has said, 'Do not let Jonathan know this, or he will be grieved.' But truly as the Lord lives and as your soul lives, there is hardly a step between me and death."
> —1 Samuel 20:1-3, emphasis added

What does it mean though, to find favour with someone? To find favour, *chên* in Hebrew, is to be acceptable to another, to extend grace. Jonathan was favourable towards David and was graceful in all his interactions with him. He chooses benevolence over malevolence, blessing over cursing, selfless love over selfish lust. It was exampled in his actions and his words and was a wilful decision.

The word first appears in Genesis 6:8 when it is written, "Noah found favor in the eyes of the Lord." Grace is an attribute of YHWH that is communicable with His creation and that which we can emulate, as did Jonathan. In Exodus 34:6 we read, "The Lord, the Lord God, [is] compassionate and gracious." YHWH is full of grace (cf. John 1:17). Grace is His favour, His blessing. In serving a gracious YHWH, the life of a believer should be one of graciousness, for grace has been given abundantly to them from YHWH. Different from mercy, grace is a favoured blessing given to us in spite of our sin. In this all-important New Testament theological doctrine expressed in Ephesians 2:8-9, grace is again spoken of and is tied to the notion of being salvific and from the hand of YHWH. In acknowledging the grace of YHWH, a believer must always be grateful and humble, and in turn, be gracious towards others. In the context of relationship with YHWH, the believer must understand that graciousness is being exhibited by YHWH in order to re-establish the amazing grace from Him that saved them and their responsibility to YHWH because of what He has done.

Jonathan's grace-filled favour towards his beloved friend revealed a heart that not only loved others, who, despite their failings, may not always deserve love, but also was distinct from the notion of mercy. Mercy is reactive; it is kindness shown in the wake of an act that deserved to be punished or which a penalty should have been fulfilled. This is not what is spoken of here, for David did no wrong towards Jonathan. The favour from Jonathan, the grace, was active in that it was compassion shown that was undeserving and not prompted by any act; it came as a total surprise from the receiver, a gift in the truest sense of the word.

A Friend Finds Favour in Their Friend (1 Samuel 20:3)

Jonathan showed favour towards his friend, as did David. As should we.

Akroartes and Poietes: Do you extend grace to your friends? Are you a believer known for being graceful towards others? Consider recent examples in which you have exhibited grace. Do a word study of "grace" in the Scriptures. Note examples of grace from YHWH and grace among human individuals. Articulate a clear understanding and definition of grace and write it in your Bible.

DAY 19

A FRIEND IS WILLING TO SERVE THEIR FRIEND (1 SAMUEL 20:4)

What does it mean to serve another? To be a bond-servant? Scripture, particularly the New Testament, often exhorts us to serve other believers, as demonstrated in Romans 1:1-17. The term servant in this passage (and the New Testament as a whole, for that matter) is better translated as "slave," being one that is totally loyal and obedient to his master. In using the word slave, we are not to focus on history's many atrocities that have occurred to people labelled as slaves; rather, the context here is denoting one who has been paid for because of their great cost. That is, due to the sin that entered the world and which humanity perpetuates, Messiah Yeshua came down to earth to die for those sins and "canceled out the certificate of debt... having nailed it to the cross" (Colossians 2:13-14). In this context, to be a "slave" for the Messiah is indeed a glorious honour, as to be a slave to any other would mean that we are not saved. Let us say to the Lord, like the slaves of the Old Testament, "I love my master... I will not go out as a free man" (Exodus 21:5 NIV)! Returning to the word servant, this again is a blessed title to hold, as many individuals in the Old Testament are referred to such as: Moses (Joshua 1:1; 14:7), David (Psalm 89:3; cf. 2 Samuel 7:5, 8), Elijah (2 Kings 10:10) and of course, Yeshua (Acts 3:13; Philippians 2:7). Not only were people servants, but Israel itself was referred to as "my servant whom I have chosen" by YHWH Himself (Isaiah 43:10).

In response to the passage explored in the last devotion, in which a distraught David spoke to his beloved friend about his father Saul's

A Friend is Willing to Serve Their Friend (1 Samuel 20:4)

quest to kill him, Jonathan responded with the voice of reason and simply said "Whatever you say, I will do for you" (1 Samuel 20:4). This was the heart of a servant, one for whom servanthood was a natural practise. He was willing to serve in any way that would help his beloved friend and to share his resources and self as was needed. There were no terms or conditions, stipulations, or even expectations. Jonathan could not only see the distress in his friend's eyes, but he was grieved that there was such unwarranted hatred directed at him. He bore no hate towards Saul, often sparing his life when given the opportunity to take it, and yet his life meant nothing to the King of Israel. We can only speculate as to whether Saul cultivated jealously towards David, seeing a love between him and his son that he was never able to replicate in his kingship. Yet, even though Saul was not willing to be a servant of YHWH or others he loved, David was willing to serve him and Jonathan.

It was David, not Saul, who preserved his life and that of his countrymen in killing the giant Goliath. Even though we see others falsely claiming this victory in the annals of history (2 Samuel 21:19; cf. 1 Chronicles 20:5), we know the truth, as documented in 1 Samuel 17 and even outside of the Scriptures (the apocryphal Wisdom of Sirach 47:4-5; Psalm 151:6-7). As such, it is not inconceivable to assume that Jonathan was more than willing to serve the one who had spared his life, as determined by YHWH. He was willing to be in the service of his believed friend, when needed or requested, and David did the same.

Akroartes and Poietes: Do you consider yourself a bondservant, a slave, for Yeshua? In doing so, how would you explain that to another believer? How are unbelievers slaves to the world? Are you willing to serve your friend when they are in need? Create a list of how you can

A Friend is Willing to Serve Their Friend (1 Samuel 20:4)

serve your friend(s) in the future, in addition to creating a list of how your friends can serve you when they ask how they can help you in the future.

DAY 20

A FRIEND IS UNWILLING TO LIE
(1 SAMUEL 20:9)

Believers are commanded by YHWH not to lie, for that is the language of Satan (John 8:44 cf. Genesis 3:1-5). The ninth of the Ten Commandments reads "You shall not bear false witness against your neighbour" (Exodus 20:16). YHWH later adds, "You shall not bear a false report; do not join your hand with a wicked man to be a malicious witness. You shall not follow the masses in doing evil, nor shall you testify in a dispute so as to turn aside after a multitude in order to pervert justice; nor shall you be partial to a poor man in his dispute" (Exodus 23:1-3). Children growing up in Israel were taught from an early age, "There are six things which the Lord hates, Yes, seven which are an abomination to Him: Haughty eyes, a lying tongue, and hands that shed innocent blood, a heart that devises wicked plans, feet that run rapidly to evil, *a false witness who utters lies*, and one who spreads strife among brothers" (Proverbs 6:16-19; emphasis added). All this would have been taught to Jonathan and David growing up.

Jonathan, consistent in his godly character, was aware of the dangers lying could bring. He could have lied numerous times in his life. For example, he could have lied to cover up that he had eaten honey despite the vow of his father that none in the land were to do so (1 Samuel 14:24-30). However, this would result in lying to five individuals: YHWH, Saul, the nation of Israel, Samuel (the author of 1-2 Samuel), and himself. If you include believers, reading of his exploits after his passing, the number grows exponentially. As such, lying is not the harmless act the world declares. White lies amassed are what build mountains of deception. Lying between one human being and another defrauds them of the truth they deserve. Lies imprison the consience, whereas the truth will always set free (John 8:32), for even if it hurts, true healing can take place.

Upon detailing his request to Jonathan as to what he should say to his father Saul about him and his desire to kill him, Jonathan replied swiftly, "Far be it from you! For if I should indeed learn that evil has been decided by my father to come upon you, then would I not tell you about it?" (1 Samuel 20:9). There is a slight tone of surprise in this question, as if to imply that to tell the truth is all that he could do as a believer and beloved friend. Even so, Jonathan was not willing to lie to his friend. What would that accomplish? Perhaps, it may have calmed David's nerves for the briefest of moments, but the cost would have been too high; it would weaken any trust between the two, and, the more one lies, the more one is untrustworthy. Jonathanl, though, was a man who was honest before any man or woman. As exampled above, the truth about him eating honey, while briefly endangering his life, resulted in a respect and support of Israel and preserving of his life. In being honest and rejecting lying as an option, his reputation preceded himself, and he became known as one who could be trusted. The bond between Jonathan and David is an example of the kind of friendship we should strive for—one in which falsehoods are degraded and truth is elevated.

Akroartes and Poietes: How serious do you see lying? Do you believe it is acceptable to lie in order to preserve perceived peace or in a desire not to hurt others? Why is this not a biblical view? If you have recently lied, confess your sin to YHWH and seek to restore a friendship founded on truth towards a friend you may have lied to. Discuss with you friend the importance of telling the truth at all times and why lying is defrauding one another of honesty.

DAY 21

A FRIEND WILL LAY DOWN THEIR LIFE FOR THEIR FRIEND (1 SAMUEL 20:13)

In 1 Samuel 20:13, we read in the Scriptures the following by Jonathan: "If it please my father to do you harm, may the Lord do so to Jonathan and more also, if I do not make it known to you and send you away, that you may go in safety. And may the Lord be with you as He has been with my father."

Jonathan was a friend that was willing to lay down his life for his beloved friend. "Greater love has no one than this, that one lay down his life for his friends" (John 15:13). This powerful verse depicts the lengths a believer will go to show the love of YHWH to another. Contextually, it applies to a mindset all believers should possess, and it is most exemplified in the leaders of the universal Assembly throughout the history of believers.

The greatest example of self-sacrifice by a leader is none other than Yeshua the Messiah. His death on the cross at Calvary, as a substitutionary atonement, reveals the cost and lengths those in leadership are willing to go to. Biblical leaders are consistent in their beliefs and teachings, wherever it takes them, even if that means prosecution, imprisonment, or even death. Decisions are made lovingly and selflessly. Truth is the currency of the rich.

This is also seen in the life of Stephen, whose martyrdom did not deter him from teaching and preaching the truth. A respected leader in the early assembly, one that he equated with the "ecclesia in the wilderness" (Acts 7:38) during the exodus from Egypt, his confrontation with other leaders who sought not the kingdom of YHWH but their own, revealed his sacrificial nature. He was willing to be the conduit for change. Even while dying, he echoed His divine leader Yeshua in how to respond to enemies with love. The case could be made that his death before Paul, who would become an apostle of the faith he once persecuted, influenced Paul to spend much of his early ministry with Jewish leaders, much like Stephen had done in his attempt to share the good news. Paul became a leader who, after Yeshua Himself, is considered the greatest model of leadership in the entire New Testament, and whose letters have been an invaluable source in constructing what a leader is according to YHWH. His self-sacrifice, depicted through his many trials and tribulations (cf. 2 Corinthians 11:23-28), shows a model of leadership in which the glory of YHWH can be achieved under any circumstances as much as at any personal cost. The good news of Messiah Yeshua saves lives, and sharing that requires sacrifice—not just finances, resources, and time, but mental and physical labor.

Jonathan, Yeshua, Stephen, Paul, and countless others declare with their words and lives that being self-sacrificing can be a defining and formative aspect of leadership. Today, many leaders in the local assembly seek to avoid sacrifice, whether in word or deed. As the contemporary Assembly endures greater oppression and persecution each and every day, it allows the separation of the wheat from the tare, the sheep from the goats, and those leaders who are Messiah's and are willing to follow and endure anything for Him, and those who are not. While sacrificing self does not automatically mean one must die for one's faith, it does mean that one must embrace a mindset that is prepared to do whatever YHWH allows and a selflessness that places the spiritual wellbeing of others before one's self. Leaders who invest their all bring greater glory for YHWH and are not deterred by what they have to sacrifice now before what is promised in eternity.

A Friend Will Lay Down Their Life For Their Friend (1 Samuel 20:13)

Akroartes and Poietes: How much are you willing to sacrifice for your friend? Would you consider giving them one of your organs if they were in need, or lend them money? Where is your line? Read the Scriptures and learn about the substitutionary atonement of Messiah Yeshua, your greatest friend. Study and commit this truth to your heart.

DAY 22

A FRIEND KEEPS THEIR VOWS (1 SAMUEL 20:17)

To vow or not to vow, that is the question. Matthew 5:33–37 suggests we are not to take oaths, but are they the same as vows? In many ways, they are the same thing, yet oaths appear to be communal in nature, before and between others, whereas vows are directly towards YHWH alone. Vows couldn't have been condemned, for the apostle Paul made one during his ministry (Acts 18:18). As for oaths, Yeshua declared that they are unnecessary for honesty and truth in character, and one's word should be sufficient; let your yes be yes and your no be no. As such, while vows can be practised today, oaths should not.

In 1 Samuel 20:12-17, we read of a vow made by Jonathan:

> Then Jonathan said to David, "The Lord, the God of Israel, be witness! When I have sounded out my father about this time tomorrow, or the third day, behold, if there is good feeling toward David, shall I not then send to you and make it known to you? If it please my father to do you harm, may the Lord do so to Jonathan and more also, if I do not make it known to you and send you away, that you may go in safety. And may the Lord be with you as He has been with my father. If I am still alive, will you not show me the lovingkindness of the Lord, that I may not die? You shall not cut off your lovingkindness from my house forever, not even when the Lord cuts off every one of the enemies of David from the face of the earth." So Jonathan made a covenant with the house of David, saying, "May the Lord require it at the hands

A Friend Keeps Their Vows (1 Samuel 20:17)

of David's enemies." Jonathan made David vow again because of his love for him, because he loved him as he loved his own life.

—1 Samuel 20:12-17

While the word covenant does not appear in the original manuscript, it can be safely assumed that this was implied by Jonathan, and a reiteration of what he made with David in 1 Samuel 18:3 (and referred to again in 1 Samuel 23:8). Jonathan calling on "Lord, the God of Israel, be [my] witness" in verse twelve affirms that he understood his covenant with David as being a vow before YHWH, not an oath made with him. While similar, the distinction is important. As much as Jonathan loved his friend David, he knew that both were sinners, and sin is unfaithful. However, YHWH is ever faithful, and he knew that any contract between men was likely to fail. However, a vow before YHWH was far likely to succeed, especially if He was receptive and blessed the individuals, which He had clearly demonstrated in the lives of both Jonathan and David. This is not to say that we should automatically assume that any covenants and vows made before YHWH will always work out, but we must have faith and not be double-minded in believing that He can't or won't work in us and see the terms of what we desire in our heart to come to fruition. Today, when a man marries a woman, they are making a covenant between one another and a vow before YHWH: two sinners, before a perfect YHWH. The intention is to remain true to the words spoken, but in being imputed with permissive will, only the omniscient YHWH knows if you will live them out, and only an omnipotent YHWH blesses those who do so, day by day.

Jonathan intended to keep his covenant with David and vow before YHWH. Will you?

Akroartes and Poietes: Revisit your thoughts and notes about covenantal love from earlier in the devotional. If you wrote a covenant with you friend, reread it and thank the Lord for such a friend. If you were hesitant to create a covenant with your friend, seek to address your barrier. It will ensure you are able to "knit" your soul to one another. Consider whether you are in a place to make a vow with your friend regarding a specific goal or issue. Do not take it lightly, but ensure it is scriptural and soaked in prayer.

DAY 23

A FRIEND GRIEVES OVER THEIR FRIEND'S MISFORTUNE (1 SAMUEL 20:34)

After being called by his father Saul the "son of a perverse, rebellious woman" (1 Samuel 20:30) and threatened that "as long as the son of Jesse lives on the earth, neither you nor your kingdom will be established" (1 Samuel 20:31), Jonathan came to the realisation that nothing he said would deter his father from wanting to kill David. And when Saul "hurled his spear at him to strike him down, Jonathan knew that his father had decided to put David to death" (1 Samuel 20:33). In processing this news, 1 Samuel 20:34 tells us that Jonathan "arose from the table in fierce anger, and did not eat food on the second day of the new moon, for he was grieved over David because his father had dishonored him."

A best friend was grieving over his beloved friend's misfortune. Believers are to "[r]ejoice with those who rejoice, and weep with those who weep" (Romans 12:15), for there is a "time to weep and a time to laugh; [a] time to mourn and a time to dance" (Ecclesiastes 3:4). The news broken to him, while intended for another, was if it has been about him personally. When you love someone, whether spouse, children, parents, or extended family, it hurts when they hurt. Sadness is emulated, as is joy, as the season dictates. The same should be true for friends. It is not done out of compulsion or in pity, it is done intentionally and willingly. It is not a grief that is fleeting or empty, as some are prone to do in promising a prayer as if it were a token gesture; it is a grief that results in a reaction both mental and physical, whether circumstantial depression, the inability to eat, the deluge of

A Friend Grieves Over Their Friend's Misfortune (1 Samuel 20:34)

tears, or planting your knees on the floor in prayer before the throne of grace (Hebrews 4:16).

It important to discuss the word anger here, for Jonathan expressed it in light of his encounter with his father Saul. Anger is an emotion of which there are two types described in Scripture: righteous anger (Mark 3:5, John 2:13-18; Ephesians 4:26) and unrighteous (Proverbs 14:17,29; Ephesians 4:26-27; James 1:20). The first is sourced by holiness, the latter by sin. The former is motivated by a grievance that the commandments of YHWH will be challenged or misappropriated, the latter is a selfish motivation that seeks only to glorify the will and appease violence. Jonathan then was expressing a righteous form of anger, one that was not cultivated in sin but rather a righteous reaction, and selflessly grieved that YHWH, His commandments, and His believing children were being sinned against.

We will soon explore the grief David expressed over his beloved friend Jonathan, but for today, it is important to highlight that the ability to grieve over a friend's misfortune is only possible if there is a deep and holy love for them. A type of empathy, to grieve for a beloved friend regardless of whether you can relate, is to have adopted a way of thinking in which you see yourself as one of countless atoms in the Body of Messiah—for if one part of the body hurts, the whole body responds.

Akroartes and Poietes: Consider when you have been righteously and unrighteously angry in your walk of faith. Have you ever been so with you friend, and was it addressed biblically? Also, have you ever found yourself grieving for your friends' misfortunes? Intentionally mourn and weep, appropriately, when your friend(s) suffer misfortune and cry out to the Lord in prayer to comfort them. If appropriate, comfort them physically.

DAY 24
A FRIEND HAS LONG-TERM VISION OF THEIR FAMILIES BEING TOGETHER
(1 SAMUEL 20:42)

In the wake of the news from Jonathan that his father Saul wanted to kill him once and for all, David had a private moment with Jonathan. Here we see how much David loved his dear friend, eliciting a heartfelt response from Jonathan as detailed in 1 Samuel 20:41-42:

> David rose from the south side and fell on his face to the ground, and bowed three times. And they kissed each other and wept together, but David wept the more. Jonathan said to David, "Go in safety, inasmuch as we have sworn to each other in the name of the Lord, saying, 'The Lord will be between me and you, and between my descendants and your descendants forever.'" Then he rose and departed, while Jonathan went into the city.
> —1 Samuel 20:41-42

It is beautiful to see David's emotions here: "David wept more." While we primarily read of Jonathan's thoughts and words for his beloved friend throughout the book of 1 Samuel, here we see that the love was equally shared and reciprocated. In praying, he placed YHWH first, then he proceeded to find solace in his beloved friend. Like all believers, he loved YHWH first and foremost and then loved others, those made in His image, as he loved himself.

A Friend Has Long-Term Vision of Their Families Being Together (1 Samuel 20:42)

Moved by the tears of his friend, Jonathan appealed to the same YHWH he also loved first and foremost and stated that the "Lord will be between me and you, and between my descendants and your descendants forever" (1 Samuel 20:42). Take pause and consider the gravity of this declaration. While Jonathan had no way to know that any of their descendants would be believers, let alone have their families remain unified, he trusted the Lord and entrusted him the desire and long-term vision of his and David's families being together. He believed that, if the foundation was strong, being YHWH Himself and thus eternal, then any families that believed in Him and loved one another as they loved themselves would be forever together. As I have often remarked among fellow believers, if we truly believe we are saved and those that are in our local assembly are equally saved, then there is no reason why we cannot begin to deepen our walk of faith with one another and knit one another's souls together now rather than when we get to Heaven. This foreign and unbiblical view of delaying intimate fellowship with beloved friends has caused a great disservice to the Body of Messiah and reveals a sadly low view of ecclesiology. Does the intimacy preserved in Scripture for marriage, or the local assembly, commence once we are in Heaven or right now? Obviously, *no*, but many people seem to view friendships in such a way, as if to suggest that some friendships are fine, just not too many, and certainly not too deep. Scripture teaches otherwise. It speaks of depth today, not tomorrow, here, not far away. It speaks of seeing generations coming to know the Lord personally as their Lord and Saviour and a vision of "all the families of the earth will be blessed" (Genesis 12:3).

Akroartes and Poietes: Do you know your friend's family? Who are they to you? Do you know of their interests and needs and about their walk of faith? How have you been involved in their lives? Be

A Friend Has Long-Term Vision of Their Families Being Together (1 Samuel 20:42)

intentional about spending time with your friend's family. Arrange regular gatherings in which both families may invest into one another and get to know one another.

DAY 25
A FRIEND ENCOURAGES IN YHWH (1 SAMUEL 23:16)

As Saul pursued David and sought to end his life, a perceived threat to his kingship with echoes of jealously in the relationship he shared with his son Jonathan, we read in 1 Samuel 13:15-16 that "David became aware that Saul had come out to seek his life while David was in the wilderness of Ziph at Horesh. And Jonathan, Saul's son, arose and went to David at Horesh, and encouraged him in God."

Encouragement. One of the most powerful and precious gifts a believer can give another. However, we encourage one another not in the things of the world, but in YHWH. Not from, not by, because of, but "in." The word "in" does not appear in the Hebrew, but the context infers Jonathan is encouraging David to pour himself into the one who alone can make him complete.

To be "encouraged... in God" speaks of sanctification. Sanctification, according to Scripture, is a godly process (which takes place after justification; Romans 3:21-26; cf. Romans 5:18-19) in which we become mentally, physically and spiritually separated from the world as we grow in the truth of YHWH (1 Corinthians 1:30; cf. John 17:16). As Christians, we are to be a "holy nation" (1 Peter 2:9), striving for peace and holiness (Hebrews 12:14) and to be holy in all our conduct (1 Peter 1:15). Through sanctification, we are being transformed into the likeness of the Son (Romans 8:28-29; cf. Hebrews 10:10). Sanctification, then, is working towards glorification (1 Corinthians 15:53; 2 Corinthians 3:18). To be "in" YHWH, "in" Messiah.

The idea of being "in" Messiah, speaks of the doctrine of being in "union with Messiah" in that we are one in Messiah. Messiah's sacrifice and atonement justified us, began a process of sanctification, and will ensure our future glorification. Those who are saved are becoming more like Messiah, and, before the Father, we could not be more loved and welcomed. By being in union with Yeshua, we partake and inherit the awe and splendour that comes with the relationship between God the Father and God the Son. It is this promise that the believer must focus on: who they are in Messiah now and who they will be in Messiah in the hereafter. YHWH both commands and desires us to change willingly and when enacted in accordance with His will and ensures that this is possible by way of His Holy Spirit, His Word and His Assembly.

Sanctification draws upon both the jubilations and tribulations of life (cf. Romans 8:28). Jonathan and David reminded one another of this, as we see in 1 Samuel 13:15-16. While YHWH did not cause David's pain, He was by his side through it all and ensured that at the end of it, "goodness" reigned. In doing so he could have gone on to become wiser, stronger, or more experienced, closer to YHWH or His Assembly, be able to forgive someone or be used by YHWH in leading someone to salvation. YHWH would ensure that He was not only victorious over the pain, but that He Himself was glorified through David. In order for this to have taken place though, David worked through pain, as we must. That may seem ludicrous to the world outside Christianity, but through the eyes of a Christian, it is a testament not only to YHWH's love and power, but ensures Satan's kingdom is divided against itself (Mark 3:24-26). By going through pain, *you are collaborating with YHWH in bringing down Satan's reign* which began over six thousand years ago in the Garden of Eden. Sharing thanksgiving and testimony in the wake of suffering is like receiving news from the frontline. It matters not that it did not involve us directly, for we are to be joyful and pleased to hear the war

A Friend Encourages in YHWH (1 Samuel 23:16)

against sin and Satan is being won. This is all possible when a believer encourages another in YHWH not away from Him.

Akroartes and Poietes: Consider what it means to be "in Messiah" and how this salvific union delights your soul. Contact at least one friend today and encourage them. If you prefer not to call them directly, send them a text or card expressing this.

DAY 26

A FRIEND KEEPS THEIR VOWS (1 SAMUEL 23:18)

This is the third reiteration regarding the covenantal love of Jonathan and David and the vow made therein. The Scriptures state in 1 Samuel 23:18, "So the two of them made a covenant before the Lord; and David stayed at Horesh while Jonathan went to his house."

The Scriptures, from Genesis to Revelation, reveal to us that YHWH highly values the role of covenant between Him and His people. Covenants are relational in nature and while not unique only to the ethnic Hebrews, those covenants established by YHWH were a source of inspiration and strength to those who were called to lead His people. As mentioned several days ago, a covenant is a formal agreement meaning "to cut" (cf. Genesis 15) and could either be conditional or unconditional in nature. Covenant loyalty is a striking feature in leadership, as it is not only exhibited by the leaders of the nation, but by every member that is a parent. This dual responsibility is best exampled in the Shema, which comes from the Mosaic Covenant.

The "Shema", a daily prayer amongst the Israelites that continues even today, begins with the well-established monotheistic revelation: "Hear, O Israel! The Lord is our God, the Lord is one!". The God of the Israelites, who has been with them from the beginning, protecting, preserving, and punishing them over countless centuries and thereon, makes known through the prophet Moses He is one. He is not one of many, one with them, or composed of many; He alone is God and the world will know Him. This theme of monotheism continues throughout the Old Testament. Regardless of what other

A Friend Keeps Their Vows (1 Samuel 23:18)

religions proclaim, their gods are not gods like He is (Psalm 82:1-8) and are non-existent before Him (Exodus 32:1; Deuteronomy 32.21; 1 Kings 18:25-29; Daniel 5:4). The central theme of the entire Old Testament is the monotheistic YHWH of Israel. As such, in regards to the Shema, the verses thereafter (6:5-9) highlight this responsibility to YHWH. We even see the "Shema" echoed in the New Testament (1 Corinthians 8:6). It is a truth we should daily recite.

It is interesting that the Shema is referred to in relation to the greatest commandments, cited and believed in by generations of believers throughout the centuries. The true "one" in our lives, is the "One" and only Lord (cf. Isaiah 42:1; Luke 23:35). In Mark 12:28-33, we read:

> One of the scribes came and… asked Him, "What commandment is the foremost of all?" [Yeshua] answered, "The foremost is, 'Hear, O Israel! The Lord our God is one Lord; and you shall love the Lord your God with all your heart, and with all your soul, and with all your mind, and with all your strength.' The second is this, 'You shall love your neighbor as yourself.' There is no other commandment greater than these." The scribe said to Him, "Right, Teacher; You have truly stated that He is One, and there is no one else besides Him; and to love Him with all the heart and with all the understanding and with all the strength, and to love one's neighbor as himself, is much more than all burnt offerings and sacrifices.
> —Mark 12:28-33

We are only able to love others and build deep friendships, because we are loved by YHWH and we love Him first and foremost.

A FRIEND KEEPS THEIR VOWS (1 SAMUEL 23:18)

That first love here makes the second love possible. Any relationship and friendship will only work when we understand that YHWH alone completes us. In establishing a covenant with David, while not made *with* YHWH, it was *before* YHWH and as such, within the parameters of what a vow is as Scripture defines it. It was a vow that he kept until death and upheld even after he was buried by his best friend.

Akroartes and Poietes: If you haven't already, memorise Mark 12:28-33 and 1 Corinthians 8:6. List the ways you can love the Lord with all your heart, soul, mind, and with all your strength, committing each to prayer. Do not merely be a Hearer of the Word, but a Doer.

DAY 27

A FRIEND DIES DOING WHAT YHWH HAS CALLED THEM TO DO (1 SAMUEL 31:2)

In understanding that there is no such thing as perfection in this life, other than YHWH Himself, then the lives we live, right to the last moment we enter the Lord's presence for eternity, should be lived loving Him and others. Jeremiah 29:11, a verse that is the possibly the most misinterpreted in Scripture in the last hundred years, is paraphrased into the question, "What are YHWH's plans for me?" Simple: "You shall love the Lord your God with all your heart, and with all your soul, and with all your mind... [and] You shall love your neighbor as yourself" (Matthew 22:37-40). Jeremiah 29:11 does not apply to us. Some struggle with this and insist on reiterating the popular mantra, but "God has a wonderful plan for my life"! Yes, He does; by loving Him you are gifted with salvation. Eternity in Heaven, not Hell. This is His plan. This is sufficient, is it not?

In understanding who we are to live for, YHWH, and how we are to live, *according to the Scriptures*, and why we are alive, *to share the good news of Messiah Yeshua and grow His Bride as a believing community*, we can now focus on how we are to die. We are to die doing what YHWH has called us to do.

The death of Jonathan is summarised in one verse: "The Philistines overtook Saul and his sons; and the Philistines killed Jonathan and Abinadab and Malchi-shua the sons of Saul" (1 Samuel 31:2). Nothing else is said about Jonathan. Jonathan died as he had lived: a warrior for YHWH. "How have the mighty fallen in the midst of the battle! Jonathan is slain on your high places" (2 Samuel 1:25). He was a believer, husband, father, son, and beloved friend.

YHWH called Jonathan in the same way he calls all of us. After the effectual call of salvation (John 6:44; Philippians 2:13; 2 Peter 1:3), YHWH calls us to work (cf. Genesis 2:15) and calls us to ministry in the body of believers (cf. 1 Corinthians 12:7). He calls some to marriage (cf. Genesis 2:18,24), some to singleness (Matthew 19:11; 1 Corinthians 7:7-8).

Jonathan died doing what YHWH had called him to do. David did what YHWH had called him to do. We will die doing what YHWH has called us to do. To have that sense of peace, to be secure in knowing that by loving YHWH and loving others, you are fulfilling the great commandments according to Yeshua, for they summarise the entire Law, is to live and die well. It is important then that we befriend an individual that does not think they have wasted their life, who laments over what they should have over what they do have, or is fearful of death. "But when this perishable will have put on the imperishable, and this mortal will have put on immortality, then will come about the saying that is written, 'Death is swallowed up in victory. O death, where is your victory? O death, where is your sting?'" (1 Corinthians 15:54-55; cf. Hosea 13:14). If we are believers, death does not separate us from YHWH, but it ushers us into His presence (Romans 8:38).

While at times my flesh fears dying, my spirit is enraptured by the reality of being with YHWH. David would have not thought that Jonathan wasted his life and died in vain. He would be sad and mourn for a season, but he knew where his beloved friend was going and that he had died doing what YHWH had called him to do. Jonathan was a believer, husband, father, son, and beloved friend. From pastor, president, and prime minister, to stay-at-home housewife, grocery

A Friend Dies Doing What YHWH Has Called Them to Do (1 Samuel 31:2)

clerk, and toilet cleaner, all are loved by YHWH and will live and die for the glory of YHWH doing what He has called them to do. Single, married, divorced, remarried, or widowed. We as believers have been called into salvation, to work, to minister in the local assembly and be content in the circumstances He has allowed us to be in; His grace is sufficient (2 Corinthians 12:9). To be friends with one who is complacent and secure in this truth is a blessing. Think and act the same for your beloved friend.

Akroartes and Poietes: In reading today's devotional do you agree with its view of YHWH calling you where you are? Do you believe you are living and will die doing what YHWH has called you to? When asked in the future what YHWH's plans are, mediate on or share Matthew 22:37-40.

DAY 28

A FRIEND LAMENTS
(2 SAMUEL 1:17)

"Then David chanted with this lament over Saul and Jonathan his son" (2 Samuel 1:17). At what point did we believe that a man showing emotions, crying even, was a sign or weakness? That "real" men don't cry, mourn, or lament over the loss of others, especially those closest to him? The Scriptures know not of such a man. Scriptures states that all of Israel, women and men, lamented after the Lord (1 Samuel 7:2). They again lamented when the prophet Samuel died (1 Samuel 28:3). To lament over others, especially those that you love, is to reveal a heart of love for others. While not commanded to lament beyond a season, we are to lament the passing of those we know and even don't know personally. As believers, we lament once for a believer, knowing that we will be reunited in Heaven. David knew this and knew that he would be rejoicing in the presence of YHWH with his beloved friend and many family members and countless believers. As believers, we lament twice when the one who has passed is an unbeliever, for theirs death is both physical and spiritual (Revelation 2014,21:8). Scripture is unclear whether King Saul was saved, but David still lamented for him.

To be and know a friend that is so centred in their faith, in control of their emotions, and laments for all that pass away, is desirable. David wrote several psalms of lament, revealing a man who loved YHWH and loved people and was grieved when either were attacked and with the latter, when they died. While we are dust and will return to dust (Genesis 3:19), we are made in the image of YHWH (Genesis 1:27). That means we have worth, have value.

A Friend Laments (2 Samuel 1:17)

To lament is to invite sympathy. We have all experienced the loss of another. Sympathy is different from empathy. While the word empathy does not appear in Scripture, the notion of sharing in one's emotions and feelings are; to clarify, empathy is concern that is absent of experience, while to be sympathetic is to have experienced to some degree what is being shared. Through YHWH, the Apostle Paul remarked: "Bless those who persecute you; bless and do not curse. Rejoice with those who rejoice, and weep with those who weep" (Romans 12:14-15). The Apostle Peter also speaks of the need to be sympathetic to believers (2 Peter 3:8-9).

To be able to sympathize (and when appropriate, empathize) with a friend is important, for a lamenting friend must not only feel safe with their friend, physically and in sharing their deepest thoughts and willingness to be corrected on their flaws and mistakes, but equally, that the other friend is Messiah-centered and is able to sympathize with them and willing to involve themselves in their lives. The application of truth, however, must reign over the involvement of emotions. The sympathetic friend must not appease the emotional demands of the lamenting friend and simply become a person to vent to and in turn, appeal to their sensitivities. The sympathetic friend needs to establish involvement with their friend by praying with them, listening to them identifying problems with them, giving biblical explanations with them, and creating solutions with them. Messiah Yeshua sympathizes with his followers (Hebrews 4:15). This is not to say He is not empathetic, but His role was to address, not cultivate, the problems.

David was a friend who lamented. It is one of his most distinguishing characteristics. Jonathan also grieved and lamented for his beloved friend, often when he was being pursued by his father Saul. To lament is to show that your heart is able to sympathise with others. It is reflective of the redeemed heart (Ezekiel 36:26).

A Friend Laments (2 Samuel 1:17)

Akroartes and Poietes: How have you shown both sympathy and empathy towards friends, past and present? Do a word study on "lament" in the Scriptures. Note examples of lamenting among human individuals. Articulate a clear understanding and definition of lamenting.

DAY 29
A FRIEND WILL RECALL A FRIEND RIGHTEOUSLY
(2 SAMUEL 1:17-27)

We come to one of the most beautiful poems, distinctly human in the way it focuses on the friendship and love between two creations of YHWH, in 2 Samuel 1:17-27. So precious to all those who read and heard of it, that it was also preserved outside of the Scriptures, in a book lost to the annals of history called the book of Jashar (2 Samuel 1:18; cf. Joshua 10:13). Lamenting over Jonathan as well as his father Saul, despite all the emotional and physical violence shown towards him, David instructed the "sons of Judah" to learn and remember it. Entitled "the Bow," it appears this was in reference to Jonathan's weapon of choice. This was most symbolic, for the bow was a weapon that required skill. It had to be created from scratch, handled with care, cultivated with patience, and the right amount of strength was to be applied when necessary. Qualities, much like a friendship fostered in love:

> "Your beauty, O Israel, is slain on your high places!
> How have the mighty fallen! "Tell it not in Gath,
> Proclaim it not in the streets of Ashkelon,
> Or the daughters of the Philistines will rejoice,
> The daughters of the uncircumcised will exult.
>
> "O mountains of Gilboa,
> Let not dew or rain be on you, nor fields of offerings;
> For there the shield of the mighty was defiled,

A Friend Will Recall a Friend Righteously (2 Samuel 1:17-27)

The shield of Saul, not anointed with oil.

"From the blood of the slain, from the fat of the mighty,
The bow of Jonathan did not turn back,
And the sword of Saul did not return empty.

"Saul and Jonathan, beloved and pleasant in their life,
And in their death they were not parted;
They were swifter than eagles,
They were stronger than lions.

"O daughters of Israel, weep over Saul,
Who clothed you luxuriously in scarlet,
Who put ornaments of gold on your apparel.

"How have the mighty fallen in the midst of the battle!
Jonathan is slain on your high places.

"I am distressed for you, my brother Jonathan;
You have been very pleasant to me.
Your love to me was more wonderful
Than the love of women.

"How have the mighty fallen,
And the weapons of war perished!"

There is so much to draw from this poem of lament, but let us focus on how David reflects on his friendship with Jonathan. He refers to him as "beloved," as being "pleasant," swift and strong. His absence causes David distress and his "love to [him] was more wonderful than the love of women." This is not homoerotic in nature or diminishing the "one in flesh" love of marriage. A husband's best friend is his wife. It is speaking of the depth of friendship, like that of a brother born of the same womb. The word "more" here is better translated as comparable to or in comparison with and "wonderful" as distinguishable or separate to. It is love, but a love in the order YHWH intended.

Akroartes and Poietes: When reflecting on your beloved friend and speaking of them to others, how do you describe them? Write it down and share it with them next time you fellowship in the Lord. Pray to the Lord and thank Him for your friends and their friendships.

DAY 30

A FRIEND WILL SHOW KINDNESS TO A FRIEND'S FAMILY
(2 SAMUEL 9:1-8)

In the aftermath of the loss of his beloved friend Jonathan, we see David showing kindness to his friend's family. He wanted to preserve for his friend a godly legacy, one that would first glorify YHWH and then showcase what trying to love others looked like:

> Then David said, "Is there yet anyone left of the house of Saul, that I may show him kindness for Jonathan's sake?" Now there was a servant of the house of Saul whose name was Ziba, and they called him to David; and the king said to him, "Are you Ziba?" And he said, "I am your servant." The king said, "Is there not yet anyone of the house of Saul to whom I may show the kindness of God?" And Ziba said to the king, "There is still a son of Jonathan who is crippled in both feet." So the king said to him, "Where is he?" And Ziba said to the king, "Behold, he is in the house of Machir the son of Ammiel in Lo-debar." Then King David sent and brought him from the house of Machir the son of Ammiel, from Lo-debar. Mephibosheth, the son of Jonathan the son of Saul, came to David and fell on his face and prostrated himself. And David said, "Mephibosheth." And he said, "Here is your servant!" David said to him, "Do not fear, for I will surely show kindness to you for the sake of your father Jonathan, and will restore to you all the land of your grandfather Saul; and you shall eat at my table regularly." 8 Again he prostrated himself and said,

A Friend Will Show Kindness to a Friend's Family (2 Samuel 9:1-8)

> "What is your servant, that you should regard a dead dog like me?"
> —2 Samuel 9:1-8

David's love did not stop with Jonathan. He loved Jonathan's family. It was a love that was intentional and thorough in that he wanted to make sure that not one member of his beloved friend's household did not benefit from their covenantal love. He inquired more than once. In doing so, he found out that Jonathan had a disabled son named Mephibosheth. He was only five years of age when his father Jonathan and grandfather Saul died in battle (2 Samuel 4:4). David, though, saw in him a fatherless child, the offspring of his most loved friend. David loved on and protected Mephibosheth, blessing him personally as he was able. While initially believing that he may have abandoned him when David was given a false report (2 Samuel 16:1-4), Mephibosheth clarified this, reaffirming his appreciation and loyalty to his father's friend (2 Samuel 9:24-30), a man whom he had come to consider his personal friend.

One of the warmest acts a beloved friend has given me, is to be "Uncle" to their children. Though not related by blood, they see me as someone they love and trust not only personally, but as a godly influence and presence for their sons and daughters. Appreciative and humbling as it is, I thank YHWH that He has cultivated in me a heart that is being conformed into the image of His Son's (Romans 8:29), a reality true for all believers. One after the heart of YHWH (cf. 1 Samuel 13:14). The blessings of YHWH and the love this ensures between two friends should not be contained; it should overflow (cf. Psalm 23:5). The husbands and wives of our beloved friends, their children and even extended family should benefit from such godly friendships. Truth be told, all godly friendships and relationships

A Friend Will Show Kindness to a Friend's Family (2 Samuel 9:1-8)

should not benefit just two people, but all those they encounter. In their character being built up and strengthened, that can only be beneficial to all those who encounter them.

The love between friends should bless those around them. Biblical love is intended to multiply and burn brightly, unlike the unbiblical love of the world that must be extinguished.

Akroartes and Poietes: How do others perceived your friendships, especially the children or extended family of your friend? Do they know of you personally, or are you a stranger to them? If your beloved friend has any children or extended family, intentionally bless them and demonstrate the work the Lord has done in your life and reflected in your friendship.

DAY 31

A FRIEND IS AN INDIVIDUAL AFTER YHWH'S HEART (ACTS 13:22)

In the Scriptures, one of the most well-known paraphrases is that "David was a man after God's heart." King David, the man YHWH chose as Israel's true king of Israel, was a man who sought and lived in accordance with YHWH's heart, the divine seat of His desires and will.

Sinner though he was, David abided by the will of YHWH, the best a sinner is able to do this side of Heaven. When he didn't abide by it, he repented and restored his desire to align his heart with that of YHWH. The often-cited paraphrase above was meant to be seen as a statement encompassing David's entire life and that, despite his appalling sins, sins, he was a man who was repentant, open to the discipline of YHWH, and sure that nothing in his life was good save that which was YHWH in him. Of all kings, all leaders, it was through David that the "Davidic Covenant" (cf. 2 Samuel 7:8-16) would be established. Before YHWH, this was the only leader that was "after [His] own heart" because of who was before his reign, during his reign, and after his reign in Israel.

The phrase first occurred in 1 Samuel 13:14: "But now your kingdom shall not endure. The Lord has sought out for Himself a man after His own heart, and the Lord has appointed him as ruler over His people, because you have not kept what the Lord commanded you". The context here is conversation between the prophet Samuel, on behalf of YHWH, with the king of Israel as chosen by the people, Saul. Here, Samuel reveals that YHWH is seeking out "a man after

His own heart", which the narrative would later reveal is David. It is also important to note that the one after the heart of YHWH will keep the commandments of the Lord, not break them or be unrepentant if they are broken (unlike Saul throughout his years of kingship).

The next reference to David being a man after the heart of YHWH is in Psalm 31. Here, David reveals his love for the Lord and a continually repentant heart. He declares YHWH as his "rock and my fortress" (v.3), admits that YHWH has "seen my affliction; You have known the troubles of my soul" (v.7), that his sin has caused his strength to fail (cf. v. 10) and he is in need of saving (cf. v. 15-16). He declares "love the Lord, all you His godly ones! The Lord preserves the faithful and fully recompenses the proud doer. Be strong and let your heart take courage, all you who hope in the Lord" (v.22-23). Like the Apostle Paul (cf. 1 Corinthians 4:16, 11:1), David desires believers to emulate his YHWH-centred heart. This psalm typifies David's love for the Lord and His commandments.

Psalm 51 is another example, being a psalm written and sung after David's adultery with Bathsheba (cf. 2 Samuel 11:2-5). Here, though breaking the commandments of YHWH, David wept over his sin and repented, asking for forgiveness. He accepted the consequences of his actions. Unlike Saul, who also broke the commandments of YHWH, David sought restoration, seeking the heart of YHWH and confessing his own (Psalm 51:1-4). David calls out "Create in me a clean heart, O God, and renew a steadfast spirit within me" (Psalm 51:10). He knows his heart does not align with that of YHWH, and He is asking Him to do what is necessary in order for justice to be appeased and peace to be restored. David understands that if he truly is repentant over his sin, his sorrow must but put into action. He must give YHWH his all: "The sacrifices of YHWH are a broken spirit; a broken and a contrite heart, O God, You will not despise" (Psalm 51:17).

A Friend is an Individual After YHWH's Heart (Acts 13:22)

Centuries later, in the wake of the life, death, and resurrection of the one promised in the Davidic Covenant, Yeshua the Messiah, His disciples would go on to spread the salvific gospel. In Acts 13:20-23, the apostle Paul testified at Antioch in Pisidia of Yeshua by briefly surveying the history of Israel. He remarked "[God] gave them judges until Samuel the prophet. Then they asked for a king, and God gave them Saul the son of Kish, a man of the tribe of Benjamin, for forty years. After He had removed him, He raised up David to be their king, concerning whom He also testified and said, 'I have found David the son of Jesse, *a man after My heart, who will do all My will.*' From the descendants of this man, according to promise, God has brought to Israel a Savior, [Yeshua]" (emphasis added). Here, David's love for the heart of YHWH is recounted as historical truth and for all generations thereafter to remember and be inspired by.

It is worth mentioning, in passing, that others saw this godly heart as well. It is interesting to contrast the opinion of YHWH of David as being a man after His heart with the reputation David had with the Gentile king in 1 Samuel 29. King Achish "found no fault" in David (v.3) and did not believe he was a man who would betray him and his forces, as did the Philistine commanders (v.4). In fact, it grieved him to request David's absence as they entered warfare (v.6-7). David's actions even verify Achish's evaluation, as he willingly accepts the request and humbly leaves (v.11). David was a man who would be betrayed in his life. 2 Samuel 15 recounts Ahitophel's betrayal (later recounted in Psalm 41). David was not one to do so. He was humble, in his youth (1 Samuel 17:39) and into his later years (2 Samuel 7:18). Recall also the reflective nature of Psalm 10. The point here, is that these characteristics, these reputable qualities seen and shared before the Gentile king Achish, are the same that YHWH had of David, despite his sin and living in the land of the Philistines. Achish saw David's YHWH-centred heart.

Believers, men and women, can emulate the heart of David which YHWH loved. Such a friend is worth seeking out being such a friend is worth being found out. It is the heart that He redeemed (Ezekiel 36:26).

Akroartes and Poietes: Biblically defined, what does it mean to be an individual after YHWH's heart? How have you reflected this in your own walk of faith, and where are you lacking and needing to strengthen your character? Reread 1-2 Samuel and then read 1 John alongside a good Bible commentary.

CONCLUSION
FAITH AND FRIENDSHIP

As humans, we are emotional beings, and when two human beings come together, there is naturally a lot of emotion invested and exposed as they build and strengthen a biblical friendship. Emotions were created by YHWH, for He is emotional, and all are created in His image. These emotions were given so that we might be like Him. However, in the wake of the Fall (cf. Genesis 3), humanity's emotions were marred, and many were corrupted and developed into what they are today. Negative emotions themselves are directly linked to the heart, the main source, and therefore, in order to deal with such emotions, it is the heart that must be admonished and aligned with the Word and will of YHWH. By fixing the heart, the emotions will adjust. Emotions, then, must be biblically transformed. Those that are addressed in Scripture must be identified as being righteous or unrighteous, biblically real, or a manifestation of post-biblical thought, and in accordance with Scripture as guided by the Holy Spirit. As such, the emotive response to the heart can be dealt in three ways; firstly, by determining the source, body or soul, secondly, if body, treat the body for the actual problem, and thirdly, if soul, go to YHWH and work on the heart issues.

Human beings are often dictated by our emotions. The way we think, talk, and act is usually determined by the emotion that dominates our mindset. Say, for example, you wake up this morning in a bad mood for reasons you can or cannot explain. If you allow your emotions to lord over you, you may mentally, verbally, and physically react in a manner that reflects this and are more likely than not to create a temporary barrier between you and YHWH (and His

Assembly). You may not pray, read Scripture, or fellowship because you don't feel like it. You're just too angry, disinterested, or sad. As a result, your emotions have gotten the better of you. Maybe you have found yourself saying once, "I don't feel like I have been saved" or "I could never be someone's friend". This is because of emotions. Even so-called "good" emotions can be dangerous at times, as some may be self-serving, shallow, and likely to change within a moment. This is why faith is so important. Faith is based on truth and not on emotions.

You will not find a single verse in Scripture that says your faith is emotionally based. On the contrary, it says the opposite. Pastor-teachers do a great disservice when explaining the Christian life through emotional descriptions and terminology, insinuating that those who do not feel or experience it in the same manner are somehow not Christians or weak in their faith. In the book of Romans, the apostle Paul states that "faith comes from hearing, and hearing by the word of Christ" (10:17). Hearing leads to understanding. He wrote elsewhere that "we walk by faith, not by sight" (2 Corinthians 5:7; cf. Hebrews 11:1). True faith is a gift from YHWH (Ephesians 2:8-9). We are incapable of having faith in YHWH by our own means, for the spiritually dead cannot express saving faith. Perhaps the best account of faith rooted in truth rather than emotions is found in Hebrews 11, where we read about Old Testament saints and see how faith based on truth defined each and every one of them; it was "By faith" (11:3-5, 7-8, 11, 20-23, 29-33) they "gained approval" (11:39). Good emotions can be great, but one's emotions can sometimes cause us problems, unintended or otherwise.

I want you to know that while emotions will be present, invested, and exposed, in this journey of biblical friendship, if you ensure that YHWH is your foundation, prioritize your love according to the

Scriptures and both believe and live out His scriptural truths, having faith that which He has commanded and promised is possible and will come true, then you will not only be a Jonathan, but you will have a friend like David, hopefully even more.

If I don't meet you in this life, I look forward to doing so in the new heaven and earth" (2 Peter 3:13).

APPENDIX 1
THE GOSPEL OF MESSIAH YESHUA

Research allegedly shows that the average person speaks around 7,000 words a day, with some achieving significantly more than that. Accurate or not, we cannot be charged as a society that has nothing to say, nor that we do not have the opportunity to say something. The question is, however, what are we talking about? What words are we speaking and how are they divided up throughout a day among the people we encounter?

Such questions are better answered by those that study communication, languages and sounds, however for the context of this appendix, there are questions and answers that can be stated and received by both believers and unbelievers reading this.

For the unbeliever, have you heard the gospel? That is one word I am certain you have heard. What of YHWH, the Scriptures, Yeshua the Messiah, sin, sacrifice and repentance? I am certain they are common words to your eardrums, especially if you attend an assembly that regularly preaches the gospel. Have you heard gospel presentations or the messages of evangelists in the streets about the need to acknowledge YHWH, your sin, and the need for that same YHWH to cleanse you of that sin lest you die in them and be separate from Him forever? That was the gospel you heard, and I suspect a few hundred words were used by the one speaking to you. So, now having heard of the good news of Yeshua the Messiah, how will you respond? Will you pretend to be deaf? Pretend you never heard the words to begin with or claim that you don't understand the language? That you were distracted by other sounds and words throughout the day and that the words of the Christian that shared the gospel with you were forgotten by the end of the day? Do you insist that unless you heard the words spoken of in the right way or have an emotional reaction to them, then it is not real or true to you? I would contend that with a few words, if I shouted to you to get out of the way of an oncoming car, you would hear and respond aptly. Or if I were to shout words of free money that you would gravitate to my words with precision like that of a missile! However, when giving you words—free words, words formed from love and truer than anything you can read in all the books of earth—you have chosen to ignore them. Think about them and consider their worthiness. You see the urgency of an oncoming car, but not the forthcoming wrath of YHWH. You see the riches of the earth, but not those that are stored in the Heavens above.

I am here to tell you this: words matter. The gospel matters. The Word who is YHWH matters.

For the believer, have you shared the gospel? Do the words YHWH, the Scriptures, Yeshua the Messiah, sin, sacrifice and repentance come from your mouth regularly? Have you given a gospel presentation among friends, family or a stranger or echoed the message of evangelists in the streets about the need to acknowledge YHWH, sin, and the need for that same YHWH to cleanse a person of that sin lest they die in them and be separated from Him forever? Do you know what the gospel is? Or are your words wasteful in a given day? Do you waste them talking about worldly matters that have no eternal value or only use holy words for a few hours each Sunday morning? Do you prefer to hear haughty words over holy words? Have you ever shared any of those potentially seven thousand words in a given day with someone who needs them more than they need the air they breathe? What are you talking about? You heard the gospel once, you heard the words of Scripture, and delighted in being made spiritually alive so you could understand them, apply them and live by them. Has that changed? Are those words mere murmurings now, distinct from the piercing heralds that called you onto salvation?

I am here to tell you this: words matter. The gospel matters. The Word who is YHWH matters.

Scripture states the following:

> How then will they call on Him in whom they have not believed? How will they believe in Him whom they have not heard? And how will they hear without a preacher? How will they preach unless they are sent? Just as it is written, "How beautiful are the feet of those who bring good news of good things!" However, they did not all heed the good news; for Isaiah says, "Lord, who has believed our report?" So faith comes from hearing, and hearing by the word of Christ.
> —Romans 10:14-17

How is one to respond to this? For the unbeliever, you are the one spoken of here that has "not believed." You are the one that needs "faith" so that you can believe in "the word of Christ." Having read it here, having heard it at your local assembly on a weekly basis, what will you now do? You will not always hear these words—the gospel of Yeshua the Messiah—so do not resist the words if you hear YHWH calling you to salvation. These words are important, for they speak truthfully of the one that alone will save you from sin, Yeshua the Messiah. Each word we construct into a sentence called the gospel, speaks of the Living Word, the Word incarnate, the Word made flesh.

For the believer, the passage from Romans is clear. For the unbeliever to hear, you must "bring good news of good things!" Talk—shout if need be—but use the words given to you, a portion of the thousands used every day, to speak of the lifesaving gospel of Yeshua the Messiah!

For your silence is assisting the demons who want nothing more than unbelievers to never hear the good news. Sinful silence, just as much as sinful action, will be accounted for before the throne of YHWH. The absence of holy words is just as vile as blasphemy. Speak, for YHWH has allowed you the privilege to spread the news of salvation using that which cost you nothing, as it was YHWH who created the oxygen you breathe, your throat, and your tongue. Speak!

I again say to all those listening: the gospel of Yeshua the Messiah, according to the Scriptures, is the free and good news of salvation that was secured through the incarnational birth, righteous life, sacrificial death, physical resurrection, witnessed ascension and ongoing intercession of the Lord Yeshua the Messiah. He lovingly drew us towards Him, forgave and cleansed us of our death-bound sins that once separated us from YHWH, and now indwells us with His Holy Spirit, which is conforming us into His image for YHWH's glory."

If you don't know what these words mean, ask. I and any true believer will gladly expound with more words, so there will be no misunderstanding or excuse. Of the seven thousand potential words you will encounter today, I have used just over one thousand.

It's your turn now.

APPENDIX 2
ON MENTORSHIP IN CHRISTIANITY

Mentoring, the means of training an individual in an area in which they require growth or guidance from one who has personally experienced or studied, is a working relationship that exists both within the secular world and the universal assembly. In the context of spiritual formation and Christian leadership, mentorship is one between YHWH, the mentor, and the mentoree. Mentorship differs from discipleship then, in that the latter often will take place within the confines of the local assembly (and under the supervision of its male eldership) and be primarily doctrinal in nature as it focuses on YHWH and His Word systematically, whereas the former mentorship, explores areas of general knowledge and Christian matters as the individual understands and in need of growth, both from a biblical worldview.

Mentoring is important, as it utilises the strengths of those with abilities and skills and seeks to connect them with others who desire to grow in their experience and understanding and are willing to submit to another in a way that becomes mutually beneficial to both parties; the mentorees humbles themselves, allowing them to learn from others in a way that is both authentic and practical, while the mentor humbly serves and imparts wisdom that was given to them by others and from YHWH. Mentoring can take place in various different environments, ranging from school and sport clubs to the corporate office and through local communities. The local assembly is most beneficial for mentorships to take place, because by its nature, it is a gathering of likeminded individuals, bonded and focused on Messiah Yeshua, while loving one another and seeking to strengthen and support their spiritual brethren.

Mentoring is a working relationship few ever engage in. This is not because it is not valuable, it is because few have the professionalism and sympathy to become a mentor, let alone be considered as one, while fewer allow themselves to become vulnerable and seek out help in a postmodern age that insists truth is relative and that you alone can help yourself. Thankfully, not all believe this and mentorship programs are growing, particularly in Christian environments. Mentoring someone is a true act of selflessness and love for one's neighbour.

Mentorship, how it is approached and the framework in which mentor and mentoree will operate, will naturally differ from person to person because of the individuals, their goals in being mentored and methods in the mentoring itself, in addition to the issues and topics raised within the working relationship. When the mentorship is centred on YHWH and involves believers, the dynamic changes again, as spiritual matters include the glory of YHWH, the teaching of Scriptures, and the work of the Holy Spirit in sanctification.

In implementing mentoring, three points must be taken into consideration. The first point is the importance of consistency and structure. There is a tendency when discussing personal and private matters, even in a professional setting, to lose track of time, to go "off script," and to find one's self not maintaining a regular time to conduct mentorship. This can be damaging, as it can lose momentum, weaken accountability, and, worse yet, be misinterpreted as the mentoring relationship being a low priority.

The point to be stressed here, is ensuring that there is a healthy barrier between not only the personal and professional, but ensuring that the mentor is not becoming too invested emotionally and that selfcare and if need be, debriefing, is taking place. Mentoring involves the mind and heart and as such, both need to rest, be looked after, and have time alone with YHWH.

The third point is to ensure encouragement along the way. The mentoree must know that progress is being made and the mentor is seeing the fruits of their labour. This is not the superficial type of affirmation, but it is acknowledging that there is value in the mentoring sessions and that the mentoree can testify that they are growing in their knowledge and understanding of the matters that are being discussed.

As a work colleague said to me, "Everyone has someone a little less mature and a little more mature in their lives, so we should both seek to pour into those behind us and to gain wisdom from those ahead of us. In friendship, those roles are sometimes reversed. That is part of the beauty of the relationship". YHWH willing, mentorship can be the foundation of lifelong friendships or prepare a brother or sister in Messiah with the tools to forge a biblical friendship with another.

AUTHOR'S BIOGRAPHY
BENJAMIN SZUMSKYJ

Benjamin Szumskyj has been a high school teacher for over seventeen years, most of these with students at risk. He is the author of *Fantasy, Horror, and the Truth: A Christian Insider's Story* and several secular works. He has earned a Master's Degree in Divinity from Liberty University, a Master's Degree in Biblical Studies from Moody Bible College, and is currently working on a Doctor of Philosophy (Ph.D.) in Bible Exposition. Above all, Benjamin loves YHWH as his Lord and Savior, and is happily married to Stacia and is the father of two sons, David and Noah, and a daughter, Rebekah, who he will see again in Heaven.

www.ingramcontent.com/pod-product-compliance
Lightning Source LLC
LaVergne TN
LVHW020934090426
835512LV00020B/3345